Acceleron
LEARNING

Product Access Instructions

Thank you for your purchase! This book includes access to our
suite of e-learning products. Use the access code and instructions
below to make the most of Life Experience. *Accelerated.*

COUPON CODE

Sq4JrT

SINGLE USE ONLY AT TIME OF REGISTRATION

1. Go to acceleronlearning.com and click "Log In".
2. Click the "Register with Coupon Code" button.
3. Enter the coupon code above and click "Submit."
4. Enter your information (including your institutional email
    address, like name@school.edu, if possible) and select your
    instructor or course from the drop-down menu.
5. Click the checkbox to agree to terms of service, and then click
    "Register."
6. You will be redirected to the log in page and will be sent an
    email with a temporary password (which you will be asked to
    change upon first log in).
7. Check with your instructor to see how long your access
    credentials will remain valid.

OUR BAD.

Why practical life skills are missing, *and what to do about it.*

Third Edition

Ryan Jackson
Founder of acceleronlearning.com

With contributions from:
Sarah Michaels
Rebecca R. Fredrickson
Gregg Jackson

Acceleron Learning and the distinctive
Acceleron Learning logo are trademarks
of The Acceleron Group, LLC.

Third Edition 2014

For information about custom editions, bulk pricing, and
corporate purchases, please contact The Acceleron Group, LLC
at sales@acceleronlearning.com

Manufactured in the United States of America

ISBN-10: 0985932406
ISBN-13: 978-0985932404

www.acceleronlearning.com

This book is dedicated with love
to my dad Gregg, for teaching me
to make the most of life.

TABLE OF CONTENTS

It's Not Rocket Surgery

Self-Examination Question
What is missing from your toolbox?

acceleronlearning.com

SUPPOSE TWO PEOPLE with identical education paths and GPAs attend and graduate from the same college. Fast forward ten years. One is well-adjusted in the "real world" and the other is a train wreck. Why?

McKinsey & Company's 2013 Education-to-Employment report highlights this critical question: "One of the things we learned in our research is how highly employers value 'soft skills.' But they are hard to define, distill, or express." The ambiguity faced by educators on this topic has a direct impact on job-preparedness. When asked if young people are prepared to work, 87% of U.S. educators surveyed by McKinsey say "yes" while *less than half* of students and employers agree.[1]

The premise of this book is that soft skills (or as we call them, practical life skills) are essential for success in American society. The problem is that no one has taken ownership of the education process or created a systematic approach to teaching them. As you will see, the absence of these skills creates a whole lot of individual, family, and societal grief. Why are practical life skills missing, and what should we do about it? This book was written to unpack the "why" question and offer a bundled solution to the problem, called Acceleron Learning (acceleronlearning.com).

Acceleron Learning is an online education company that teaches practical life skills and prepares people for major life decisions. We seek to influence the academic, political, and social discussions on education in America by demonstrating an effective approach to preparing people for success in the real world. What does that preparation look like? Does it include knowing how to change a flat tire? How to host a Thanksgiving dinner?

There is a certain set of knowledge and behaviors that

help people approach common life challenges with greater awareness and confidence. If you are competent in these "pillars," you will be better equipped to succeed in life. However, even smart, intellectual people can (and do!) make dumb decisions about these practical life skills:

- **Financial Literacy** – How to manage, protect, and grow your money. Examples include investing, insurance, using credit, planning for retirement, personal budgeting, basic economic theory, and how major life decisions have a financial impact.
- **Career Dynamics** – How to manage people and work to get your career on track. Examples include motivating others, defining and solving problems, project planning, preparing for interviews, and building the perfect résumé. Also included are topics that help students navigate college and effectively launch their career.
- **Legal Basics** – How the legal system works and how it impacts your professional and personal life. Examples include intellectual property, employment law, contracts, estate planning, and the legal impact of major life decisions.
- **Personal Wellness** – How to enhance your physical, mental, and social health. Examples include emotional health, balanced nutrition, building healthy relationships, and making the most of exercise.

Let's be honest. These four pillars are not rocket science or brain surgery. However, practical life skills are not taught in an organized manner, and most of the resources out there are narrowly focused and difficult to consume. For example, you can scour the Internet or visit a local bookstore and find hundreds of books on personal finance. The problem is most people don't know how to evaluate the quality of what they are reading, or how to condense a 200-page book on something dry (e.g. life insurance) into useful everyday knowledge. On the other end of the spectrum, so-called "bridge programs" are cropping up as a way to fill the gap. These month-long boot camps target students at top universities, like Harvard, and charge a hefty $5,000–$10,000 fee to teach practical life skills. Isn't it odd that after spending $200,000 to go to a top school, students must pay several thousand dollars more just to obtain basic soft skills? There is something very wrong with this picture.

The *Wall Street Journal* recently reported on these bridge programs, saying "Amid a brutal job market for graduates and growing concern that a liberal-arts education may not translate into real-world success, even accomplished students are desperate for any potential edge. Though schools have beefed up their career services in recent years, students still fear they lack the practical skills they'll need after graduation, such as deciphering a balance sheet or leading colleagues on a project."[2] Acceleron Learning teaches these topics, and many more. We offer a cost effective solution (under $99 for multiple years of individual consumer access) that is economical and accessible to anyone, not just those in the Ivy League. The marketplace has identified the need, and we offer a comprehensive solution.

Before embarking on a detailed discussion of why practical life skills are missing and what to do about it, let me give you a little more detail on Acceleron Learning's approach to teaching practical life skills. Take a topic like personal budgeting or how to manage people, and condense the "need to know" essentials into a 30-minute video lecture. Focus on immediately useful content, and include practical methods and examples. Apply that knowledge with web-based tools that provide a structured approach to managing some of life's biggest decisions. We have eliminated the guesswork and taken care of the research. Our content was developed by experts who are also practitioners. That means no egg-heads. We employed bright minds to develop the content. These are people who have worked with the world's top corporations, organizations, and academic institutions. Each product is founded on solid academic theory, but is brought to life by real-world experience. The focus is always on providing seasoned wisdom, approaches, and tools that anyone can use right away.

We want to engage people in a variety of contexts (at home, at school, and at work) with products that are designed for individual learning, classroom instruction, and professional development. We have made every effort to provide just the essentials in an easily-consumable format that keeps pace with technology. Acceleron Learning is on the web and available for mobile devices including phones and tablets. Check out the Acceleron Learning App available at the App Store and Google Play.

The value of Acceleron Learning is in the bundle: A high-quality assortment of the practical life skills you need, all in one place. With our products, you are an active participant rather than a passive recipient. The goal is proactivity. We want you to become a better steward of your life and your resources. After studying with Acceleron Learning, we believe you will:

> ▸ Understand foundations in financial literacy, career
> dynamics, legal basics, and personal wellness;
> ▸ Have a basic vocabulary in these subjects and be able
> to ask intelligent questions;
> ▸ Know when and how to seek professional advice on
> these subjects; and
> ▸ Make better decisions in life with greater confidence,
> and superior results.

The curriculum is capable of introducing concepts before they are needed, and at any age-level, from kindergarten to adulthood. Basic knowledge creates awareness and provides a framework to build upon. Knowing a little bit about a subject matter and the vocabulary that goes with it will reduce the intimidation factor, enable you to conduct deeper research on your own, and allow you to ask intelligent questions of professional advisors. Finally, understanding the interdependencies across topic areas will help you face the inherent complexity of life's challenges.

What we offer is an approach to teaching practical life skills, but it is not a golden ticket. If you can find a better solution, that's great! Our main goal is to raise awareness and enact positive change in the lives of our neighbors and society at large, however that unfolds. We are not under any false illusion that we have THE answer to the problem. But, we do have something that is thoughtful, works well, and is ready to go. So, to the college administrator, to the organization, to the parent, and to the individual: We have all passed the buck on teaching practical life skills. The book isn't called *Someone Else's Bad*. It is *Our Bad*. The good news is that Acceleron Learning was created to get you moving in the right direction in a big way. Use it. We all have to take ownership if we want things to change.

Here's some more good news. If you're reading this book because your school or organization is using Acceleron Learning, that puts them in the (refreshing) minority who understand the challenges you face every day. To be clear, they are not the object of the criticisms levied in this book. Instead, you should applaud your administrators or managers for offering practical life skills education. *They get it!*

By the way, we are not the only ones interested in this stuff. In their recent book *Wellbeing: The Five Essential Elements*, The Gallup Organization identified career, social, financial, physical, and community elements as those that most impact your wellbeing. Gallup is a global polling, consulting, and publishing company that is famous for their public-opinion and presidential election polls. In other words, they are well regarded and empirically rigorous. The elements they identified closely parallel our four pillars: financial literacy, career dynamics, legal basics, and personal wellness. *Wellbeing*, is a cornerstone of our hypothesis.

The folks at Gallup also created an assessment tool called the *Wellbeing Finder*, which measures individual and community wellbeing. The response to these dimensions is segmented into thriving, struggling, or suffering for each essential element.[3] The tool allows respondents to gauge their overall wellbeing and see which areas can use improvement. That information is available for your community at well-beingindex.com. Gallup has also recently launched a version of *Wellbeing Finder* aimed at measuring the success of college graduates, in particular, by focusing on employment status, earnings, and workplace preparation. Gallup CEO Jim Clifton explains:

"Gallup's hundreds of business clients report that many, if not most, college diplomas don't tell them much about graduates' readiness for productive work. Average grades have been inflated, and just about every business leader knows it. Degrees are increasingly awarded in subjects of questionable academic—let alone market—value. Many employers today see a diploma as something that shows a student had the brains to be admitted to college and maybe the discipline to finish. But they sure don't see those pieces of paper as proof that a graduate is remotely prepared for workplace performance or leadership."[4]

We've discussed our product with Gallup and shown it to them, and they like it.[5] However, Gallup is primarily in the measurement business, not the education business. Acceleron Learning picks up where Gallup leaves off by providing a comprehensive, bundled solution.

CHAPTER 1

Hugh Dunno

Self-Examination Question
Do you know what "Hugh Dunno"?

acceleronlearning.com

Hey, how's it going? I'm Hugh Dunno, and as you're about to find out, I could use a practical life skills tune-up. Let's see if any part of my story sounds familiar to you or someone you know.

I have always loved the arts, especially film. When I graduated from high school, I did not have a whole lot of direction in my career path, so I decided to pursue my passion. I worked on some cool projects, but breaking into the movie-making business looked pretty bleak while I was at Big U. I took my dad's advice and changed my major to business. That added another year of school, more college loans, and lost earning potential. But at least I was better positioned for the job market...or so I thought. I did not realize until after graduation that internships and relevant extracurricular activities were "must have" items to be competitive.

Anyway, after graduating from college it took me three months to land a decent job because I did not have related work experience and I struggled with interviews. It turned out that working on films is a skill many employers are not looking for. They asked me what my career goals were. Um, to get a job? Hello! As luck would have it, I finally got hired for a sales position close to home.

For the first few years the job was decent. I worked hard and rewarded myself for it. I bought a new car, rented a downtown apartment, and maxed out a few credit cards in the process. I was not keeping track of my personal budget, so the credit card debt kept piling up. I also overlooked personal investing, even though my HR department had some good information. Retirement was far off in the future and I didn't know what questions to ask, so I dismissed it.

Luckily, my hard work eventually paid off with a promotion to supervisor and a pay increase. As I moved up the career ladder, it became more difficult to meet my employer's expectations. I did not know how to manage people effectively or what constituted good business decision-making. Then, I had that little misstep with my employer's intellectual property. I just went with my gut without considering the need for legal counsel. As I found out the hard way, navigating the workplace can be difficult. An MBA might have helped, but I never knew how to assess the benefits versus the time commitment and cost of pursuing a higher degree.

By my late twenties I met Mrs. Right. Once we got married, we had to work through a difficult season where her elderly father moved in. Decisions about caring for his health, navigating estate planning, and handling our personal finances were stressful, and of course our families took sides. It would have been nice to know how to manage conflict.

This brings us to today. We have a four-year-old boy and are expecting a little girl. My wife quit working to raise our kids. We are trying to save enough money for the down payment on a house, but I'm a little intimidated about mortgages and contract law, so I'll just pay an attorney or financial advisor to tell me what to do.

I can feel my marriage approaching a tipping point. I am not getting enough sleep and I don't take time to exercise. My wife is exhausted all the time from taking care of our home and son. We don't spend time together like we used to. The financial strain of credit card debt, thoughts of planning for our retirement and the children's education are all overwhelming. Fears of bankruptcy, divorce, and being a bad parent are beginning to creep into my mind.

It pains me to think that I was so unaware and didn't ask for help earlier. Turning all of this around will take a lot of

*work. I just don't know how to get the ball rolling. I really don't
know what I don't know, and it doesn't seem that my family,
friends, or community are equipped to help.*

DOES HUGH DUNNO sound like someone you know?
Maybe a friend, coworker, or family member? Do you see
parts of yourself in Hugh Dunno? (Do you hesitate to say yes?)

You are not alone. Everyone knows someone with *at least
one of* these challenges. People have a tendency to spend beyond their means, taking on mountains of debt they can't pay
back. They don't understand the financial implications of major
life decisions like buying a car, pursing a college education, or
buying a home. When others talk about financial products like
insurance or investments, they might as well be speaking a
foreign language. Many people do not enjoy what they do in
their career. They are disengaged at work, which causes lower
productivity, mistakes, and difficulty forming good professional relationships. They don't know or fail to practice good
decision-making, interpersonal dynamics, or workplace management skills. People are often unaware that their body language, tone, physical appearance, behaviors, and thought
processes work against them, often resulting in lost opportunities and strained relationships. Many people don't understand
the contracts they sign, such as insurance policies, wills, and
work agreements. These misunderstandings get them in a
world of trouble. On top of all of that, many people just don't
take care of themselves. Poor diet decisions, little or no exercise, and no framework for proactive health maintenance
wreak havoc on their bodies and minds over the long haul.

It is easy to deny these things are happening, but denial is
not the way to go. You have to take action, which requires edu-

cation and informed decision-making. Awareness, education, and action—those are the steps.

The majority of Americans don't have the education necessary to take action! It is difficult to comprehend the benefit of having practical life skills before encountering a problem. The benefits of having the skills and the costs of not having them are cumulative. The net effect can take quite a long time to manifest. As a result, the sense of urgency is absent, and it's devastating. Had people grasped practical life skills ahead of time, they may not have ended up in a career they hate with unmanageable debt, legal trouble, or preventable illness. Sadly, practical life skills education is not mandatory in America. As *New York Times* and *Wall Street Journal* columnist Daniel Akst wrote in his book, *Temptation: Finding Self-Control in an Age of Excess*, "You can't graduate from most colleges without studying a foreign language, but you can (and probably did) emerge ignorant of [personal] financial management and nutrition."[1] The problem is not limited to those with low socioeconomic or education status. These critical skills are treated like an elective in every corner of American life, and it shows.

Don't be surprised if you, too, lack at least some (or many!) practical life skills. Who is responsible for this problem? How did this happen to America? And how do you learn what Hugh Dunno? Let's find out.

CHAPTER 2

Pointing in the Mirror

Self-Examination Question
Is it possible that we're all part of the problem?

acceleronlearning.com

IMAGINE YOU ARE hosting a dinner party. You have invited a few close friends, neighbors, colleagues, and family. The topic of practical life skills comes up. It's the stuff you don't learn in school like personal finance, managing your career, how the legal system works, and taking care of your body and mind.

You ask, "Who is responsible for teaching this stuff?" Let the blame game begin.

YOUR BOSS

I hire new employees and they aren't prepared. Their personal lives (financial, legal, physical, mental, and social) are a mess. They are technically proficient, but can't function effectively in the workplace. What are all of these colleges producing, anyway? I have to babysit and hand-hold for the first three years of their employment before they're worth anything. What's more, my tenured employees carry the baggage of bad decisions they made early in their careers. As an employer, all of this ends up in my lap. I blame higher education!

YOUR COLLEGE PROFESSOR

What are you talking about? We have resources for students: career services, deep technical training, and elective courses if they want to learn about something like personal budgeting. They just have to ask for it. If you weren't happy with the product, you shouldn't have hired the employee.

YOUR COWORKER

Hold on a minute. I didn't know that those things were available to me in college or I would have taken advantage of them. Now I'm in the working world and it's nothing like I thought it would be. I get my work done, but I don't get along with my coworkers. The other day, the administrative assistant asked me if I was okay because I seemed stressed. Well, I am! I'm over $30,000 in debt with a college degree that is irrelevant for the work I'm doing. I didn't know I needed practical life skills until I got into the workplace! Why didn't I learn how to choose the right career path and how to form good working relationships in elementary, middle, and high school? Why didn't my parents teach me this stuff when I was a kid? Why didn't my college step up and take responsibility for teaching these topics? It's like no one is looking out for my wellbeing.

YOUR DAD

Hate to admit it, but I couldn't have helped you if I wanted to. How am I supposed to teach my kid if I don't know what I don't know? Plus, I'm not the best role model because of all of the problems in my life, and I don't have a bunch of time or money to throw at the problem. I assumed it was the responsibility of K–12 education and college to prepare our kids for the real world! Exactly what have I been getting for all of these tax dollars and tuition bills?

YOUR MAYOR

Now hold on! "Tax dollars" can mean a lot of things. We only have local property and income tax dollars to work with, and that money goes towards providing basic city services. Our municipal government is concerned about the general wellbeing of residents. You know, things like infrastructure, the local economy, and public safety. We're not in the education business. This is clearly a problem for some other government agency to handle.

YOUR HIGH SCHOOL TEACHER

Well, it would be nice if we could teach practical life skills, but we can't even squeeze in the basics! Standardized testing is killing us, and even if we had space to teach something like personal budgeting, we don't have the money. We can't even meet existing financial literacy mandates imposed by state legislatures. And now you want to add career, legal, and personal wellness topics? Parents should teach this stuff to their kids! We're tired of parenting for you.

YOUR SISTER

In the end, I'm the one hurt by all of this. You know, I'm in my third year of college and I have yet to declare a major. I have no idea what my career path is, and I have no idea what I want to do with my life. I should probably start applying for jobs soon, but I don't know how to do that effectively either. Don't get me wrong, college has been really fun. I'm making new friends, staying out late, going to class (most of the time), studying abroad, and taking fantastic spring break trips, but reality is starting to hit. I have $40,000 in student loans so far. I thought I had a scholarship that would cover most of my tuition, but it never panned out. I had no idea that college would be so expensive. I have no idea how I will pay off all my student loans after I graduate...if I graduate at all.

Little bits of this conversation are happening across America every day. We all see the effects of the problem, but only in isolated pieces. The lack of practical life skills and the shotgun approach to addressing that gap is chipping away at our society and its future. But it's someone else's problem to figure out.

Wrong! It's my problem, and your problem, and her problem, and his problem, and their problem, and it's *Our Bad.*

CHAPTER 3

The Hole Problem

Self-Examination Question
Do you see a gap?

acceleronlearning.com

ACOMPELLING STATISTIC from Michigan State University clearly identifies the kind of knowledge and skills most important for success and parallels similar research from Harvard, UNC Charlotte, and others. What it ultimately reveals is a gaping hole in the structure of this nation's education system. To summarize:

> 80% of a person's success comes from soft skills and 20% comes from technical skills.[1]

Technical skills are abilities required to perform specific tasks. For example, working as an engineer, writer, or biologist requires different technical proficiencies to do the job well. Soft skills, on the other hand, are interpersonal dynamics, knowledge, and preparedness that characterize how a person interacts with the world around them. The problem is that this nation's education system puts virtually all of the emphasis on the 20%, and the remaining 80% is neglected. People may enter the working world with technical knowledge (the 20%), but that alone will not guarantee success. People need to have a range of skills to effectively handle daily interactions, decisions, and life's major events.

For argument's sake, even if the studies are way off—say that 50% of a person's success is driven by soft skills—our society is still missing the mark! You could be the most intelligent person in the world, but if you don't know how to communicate your ideas clearly and work well with others, you are at a significant disadvantage when it comes to employability:

It's because college kids today can't do math, one line of reasoning goes. Or they don't know science. Or they're clueless about technology, aside from their myriad social-media profiles. These are all good theories, but the problem with the un-employability of these young adults goes way beyond a lack of STEM skills. The technical term for navigating a workplace effectively might be soft skills, but employers are facing some hard facts: the entry-level candidates who are on tap to join the ranks of full-time work are clueless about the fundamentals of office life.[2]

"Clueless" is a pretty strong descriptor, one that should get the attention of educators. You might expect committees at school districts and colleges around the country to seize this issue and being working to solve it. After all, schools are responsible for producing the student that ultimately lands in the hands of employers. But it's difficult to solve a problem when you don't believe that there actually is a problem. This is strikingly the case, as a side-by-side comparison of statistics from *Inside Higher Ed* points out:

If provosts could grade themselves on how well they're preparing students for success in the work force, they'd give themselves an A+. They did, sort of, in *Inside Higher Ed's* 2014 survey of chief academic officers. Ninety-six percent said they were doing a good job—but they may have been grading on a curve.

In a new survey by Gallup measuring how business leaders and the American public view the state and value of higher education, just 14 percent of Americans—and only 11 percent of business leaders—strongly agreed that graduates have the necessary skills and competencies to succeed in the workplace.[3]

96% of college leaders vs. 11% of business leaders...that is an alarming gap and students are caught in the middle. But do the students themselves see the problem? Andy Chan, vice president for personal and career development at Wake Forest authored a 2013 research report showing that students and employers have very different perspectives on "business basic" preparedness. Things like "creating a budget or financial goal" and "writing to communicate ideas or explain information clearly" each show a 22 percentage-point gap, and "organization" showed a 25 percentage point gap. In the widest gap, at 27 percentage points, 77 percent of students but only half of hiring managers reported preparation for "prioritizing work." The report concluded:

Colleges aren't doing enough to prepare students for the work force. In most cases, career services is an isolated, overbooked office that can go underutilized or flat-out ignored. Instead, colleges should be embedding career development into the fabric of undergraduate education. Not only would this better prepare students for life after college, it would help to justify the value of a liberal arts degree.[4]

So employers are stuck with the proverbial bag. Janette Marx, senior vice president at Adecco Staffing U.S. calls this phenomenon a "new talent gap," and urged that a "collaborative effort by employers and educational leaders" is necessary to build a competitive workforce.[5]

On a macro level, the pervasive absence of practical life skills has created a nation that is mired by financial illiteracy, career ineffectiveness, legal illiteracy, and personal illness. The United States is plunging deeper into debt at both the government and the consumer level. The education system is not preparing students for fulfilling and stable careers. People do not understand the legal implications of their decisions, and most of us are not healthier despite having longer life expectancies.

It's old news that our society is facing these problems, but how do we bring about positive change? It requires two forces, just like the sharp blades of a pair of scissors, to effectively cut through the issues. One blade is structural change and the other is personal responsibility.

Let's first look at the obstacles in bringing about structural change. This is the "big picture" change that must be enacted by institutions like government and the powerful trade groups that represent various stakeholders in education and the labor market. Harvard economist Dani Rodrik observes:

> All sustained episodes of growth are underpinned by fundamental structural change. Of course, you can get growth spurts because of an improvement in the terms of trade or a sudden burst of capital inflows. But those tend to peter out unless there is the emergence and expansion of

new industries, and movement of labor from traditional industries into modern industries. This is the essence of structural change. Without these things happening, a country is not likely to achieve long-term growth.[6]

The issue here is that Americans do not feel they can rely on people in positions of power to help. A 2011 poll showed that confidence in the federal government is half of what it was a decade ago.[7] Politicians have become fixated on pleasing the electorate, and they spend money and make legislative decisions without the right level of prudence. Career politicians seek to keep positions of power, so they will continue to tell us what we want to hear and give us what we demand in order to do so.

It is tempting to point the finger at the system, and say that our nation's problems are the result of a broken government. There may be some truth to that, but our elected officials are just representing the interests that we the people espouse. "Society" is nothing more than you and me, and everybody else. Each election cycle, we vote people into national, state, and local government positions. They make decisions on our behalf. Or, at least that's how it is supposed to work. Getting this nation back on track requires people to be informed on the issues and vote in candidates that support those beliefs. The instrumentality to enact change exists. People just have to be informed and care enough to do something about it.

This brings us to personal responsibility, the other edge that cuts the cloth of change. Sadly, that blade is increasingly dull. Actions flow from ideals, and our culture has become both consumerist and entitled. These attitudes and beliefs are unmistakable: I want to be entertained, I should get it now, and I will be provided for. The tenacity required to build and maintain a strong nation seems to have been lost. The Greatest Generation built the wealth, the Baby Boomers maintained it for a while, and my generation is slowly squandering it. This detachment from the effort and toil has in part led my generation, the Millennials or Generation Y, to possess a sense of entitlement. Millennials' experiences inform them that we've always gotten whatever we've wanted with minimal effort.

In his cultural critique, *The Road Trip that Changed the World*, author Mark Sayers drives this point home: "In the contemporary culture the message is clear: happiness and fulfillment are found in breaking away from community, social expectations, rules, and tradition. Thus the life script of the contemporary world is to gain as much individual freedom as possible to assert one's desires, and this is achieved through escaping from relational and social expectations."[8] In short, we seem to have lost touch with reality and it shows.

My peers and I didn't grow up during a great depression, live through a world war, or experience the sociopolitical ups and downs of the 1960s, 70s, and early 80s. We were spoiled by parents who didn't want us to struggle like they did. A little bit of struggle is good, because it makes you more self-reliant and resilient. In fairness, the 2008 financial crisis in the U.S. was a wake-up call, but the misguided mentality is still largely intact. Today's youngest generations, Generation Z (born in the 1990s–2010) and Generation Alpha (born after 2010), have grown up with an expectation of immediacy and ease. The Information Age, while slick, will require us to solve big social problems. And no, there's not an app for that.

Over the next several pages, we'll take a look at some of the root causes behind our collective financial illiteracy, career ineffectiveness, legal illiteracy, and personal illness. This context is important, but if you are a "cut to the chase" kind of person, you can go to Chapter 8: Life Experience. *Accelerated.*, for the details on how Acceleron Learning offers the practical life skills education that is necessary to address these challenges. After that, we'll look at common barriers to change and explain how you can take action.

Just remember—you have to actually do something! Acceleron Learning provides a great deal of knowledge in an easy-to-consume format, designed specifically to minimize the barriers to implementation at schools and workplaces (structure!). However, you still have to put in the effort to learn and enact change (personal responsibility!)...or nothing will happen.

CHAPTER 4

Financial Illiteracy

Self-Examination Question
What financial challenges could you have
avoided with the right skills early on?

acceleronlearning.com

AS THE SAYING GOES, money makes the world go round. Good personal finance is a major contributor to stability in our society. Given the number of important and complex financial transactions faced by consumers every day, the level of financial literacy in the U.S. is staggeringly low. Broadly defined, financial literacy is the ability to properly manage, protect, and grow your money and assets, and absence of these skills are evident in the Federal Government budget and the American household budget alike.

Let's begin at the top. A 2012 poll found that the national deficit ranks only second to unemployment and job scarcity as the most critical problem in the United States. The same poll was conducted in 2011 with the same results.[1] As of the writing of this book, the United States' national debt was approaching $18 trillion and climbing.[2] An article in the Washington Times projected a deficit spending trend of $1 trillion each fiscal year through 2021.[3]

It is difficult for most people to conceptualize one trillion dollars. Hal Mason, a retired accountant with over 40 years' experience in budgets, 27 of those years with IBM, gives some perspective: "If you were to try to pay it off $1 a second—just to pay off $1 trillion would take 32,000 years."[4] If the U.S. is going to pay off its mountain of debt, many more people need to understand basic financial matters. Informed citizens can bring that knowledge to the polls, and vote for fiscally responsible candidates.

Mason pointed out the simple reason why Congress cannot balance the budget nor reduce spending: "To balance the budget, Congress would either have to raise taxes 50% or eliminate the federal government...If they cut entitlements and pensions our nation will have riots like Greece."[5]

Debt and deficit spending may be hot debate topics, but unbridled spending at the Federal level sets a tone for everything else. It's not just in Washington D.C. Financial stress is causing family units to implode. Everyone knows the rate of divorce in the United States is fast approaching 50%. What is the number one reason for divorce? Money. People do not manage their money well. They either don't understand the implication of their financial habits, or they spend regardless.

Think about it. Nearly all of us get a paycheck. We have to make decisions on how to spend our money, and how to plan for our financial future. Yet few of us have even a basic vocabulary for discussing common financial products or concepts. We've all heard of home mortgages, property insurance, mutual funds, and 401(k) plans. When you get into a conversation about these topics with friends or get ready to use such instruments, are you confident? Do you (or they) really understand underlying concepts like compound interest, fixed vs. variable expenses, or collateral? Do you understand how to create and maintain a basic personal budget?

Two economists, Annamaria Lusardi of Dartmouth, and Olivia Mitchell of the University of Pennsylvania, recently studied financial literacy in America. They asked the following questions of Americans over the age of 50, an age group that has had lots of time to become informed about basic financial concepts. Here are a few of the questions. See how you do.

1. Suppose you had $100 in a savings account and the interest rate was 2% per year. After five years how much do you think you would have in the account if you left the

money to grow: more than $102, exactly $102, or less than
$102?

2. Imagine that the interest rate on your savings account
   was 1% per year and inflation was 2% per year. After one
   year would you be able to buy more than, exactly the
   same as, or less than today with the money in this
   account?

3. Do you think that the following statement is true or false?
   "Buying a single company stock usually provides a safer
   return than a stock mutual fund."

The answers are the following: #1 (more than, due to compound interest), #2 (less than, inflation outpaces interest and results in lower purchasing power), and #3 (false, mutual funds generally create diversification, which reduces risk vs. holding the stock of a single company). An article in *Forbes Magazine* pointed out that only half of those quizzed could answer questions 1 and 2 correctly, and less than one-third answered all three questions correctly. The numbers are dismal. A similar study revealed that even fewer people correctly answered a basic compound interest problem.[6]

Most kids don't learn financial literacy in school. Only about a dozen states require some sort of personal finance instruction. Of the states that require financial literacy education, funding may be inadequate (ironic, right?) and the requirements may be vague, like "teach concepts on personal budgeting." Our kids are growing into adults who don't know how to manage their personal finances. A financial literacy survey showed that the majority of 18- to 34-year olds do not know how to keep a budget.[7] How can we expect youngsters to spend wisely when they have no idea how to balance a budget?

The United States' Secretary of Education Arne Duncan said, "'There has been a devastating cost to a lack of attention, urgency and seriousness of taking this on,'...noting that the housing crisis, low savings rate and poor retirement planning all flow out of the financial literacy issue."[8] Young people's lack of financial literacy has serious repercussions for the U.S. economy:

> Whether they're learning about managing money, or not, at home or in school, the lack of financial savvy among Millennials could have a trickle-down effect with detrimental consequences for society, experts say...And if the next generation is unable to 'continually acquire skills' [says Ted Beck, CEO of the National Endowment for Financial Education]...The United States is left with an uncompetitive and unattractive workforce that by necessity will lean more on social programs.[9]

An article in *USA Today* pointed out that "A majority of young people in the United States have poor financial literacy, a trend that has been consistent over the past decade and shows few signs of improving."[10] This is especially precarious as these young adults face "an average debt of about $45,000, which includes everything from cars to credit cards to student loans to mortgages,"[11] and "Unemployment for those 18–29 is 12.4%, well above the national rate [about] 8%."[12]

The cost of higher education has now become a huge source of debt for college students and graduates, and for our nation as a whole. Because of poor career and financial planning, students are racking up tens of thousands of dollars in college loans. Data analysis performed by the *New York Times* showed that 94% of students who graduate with a bachelor's degree borrow money to pay for their college education; this number was 45% in 1993.[13] The Project on Student Debt found that college seniors from the class of 2012 graduated with an average of $29,400 in student loan debt.[14] Today, the total outstanding student debt is over $1.1 trillion and climbing.

That $1.1 trillion of student debt comes on the heels of the housing crisis and the credit card fiasco. William Brewer, president of the National Association of Consumer Bankruptcy Attorneys, said our nation's student debt crisis has the potential "to be the next debt bomb for the U.S. economy." Free credit (easy access to student loans) drives up demand for college educations which drives up tuition. Then, just like the housing crisis, we are upside-down and have overpaid. Taxpayers are subsidizing overpriced degrees, and they stand a chance of not getting their money back. We as consumers face the possibility of paying for all of this student debt as loans are defaulted. Prior legislation has prevented bankruptcy from being an option to skirt student loan debt. Letting these loans go uncollected or allowing bankruptcy would be a huge mistake, but the pressure is mounting for consumers to have an "out." In late 2012, the U.S. Department of Education introduced a "Pay as You Earn" program. It allows eligible student-loan borrowers to cap monthly payments to 10 percent of discretionary income, and have their loans forgiven after 20 years. While such programs may seem like a good deal for struggling students, they severely undermine financial and legal structures in our society and create a perverse incentive for those borrowers to be lax about career and long-term economic decisions.

Ok, so how did we get here? In many respects, our society's

financial illiteracy goes back to the introduction of the credit card in the middle of the twentieth century. We can't blame our problems on the credit card itself. Credit as a financial tool works quite nicely. It helps transact business efficiently. The problem is that you're allowed to finance what you don't pay off at the end of the month, and therein lies the problem—credit cards allow a person to live beyond their means. Are you spending more money than you make?

The credit card took off in a major way during the 1950s, starting with the Diners Club Card.[15] Before the credit card took center stage, our society was pay as you go. But with millions of servicemen returning home after World War II there was a huge increase in demand for homes and automobiles, and people needed a way to pay for these things. That's where credit cards, mortgages, and car financing intervened. Before that, car loans were rare and were for small amounts of money. But with a lot of building and manufacturing post-World War II, companies and consumers alike needed credit to fund the demand. Not only did the credit card fill a need, it fueled consumerism (buy stuff!) by distancing people from the implications of their spending habits. Richard Thaler, an economist from the University of Chicago, explained this dissociation: "Credit cards act as a 'decoupling device' because they separate the joy of the immediate purchase from the pain of the payment, which is off in the distant future."[16] If you run out of cash, the credit card provides an instant remedy. The necessity to control your spending to stay within a budget is no longer mandatory.

Credit is best suited for long-term economic investments where you or someone will get a lot of useful life out of an asset, like a house. Credit also makes sense for assets that appreciate (that is, increase) in value. But, credit breaks down when people use it to finance things that have a very short-term economic benefit. One example is going on a vacation. Suppose you spend $1,200 on your next vacation. You come back and you have a $1,200 bill to pay. Now, only one thing has impacted your balance sheet (a statement that shows your financial health): you have $1,200 less cash. There's no asset (tangible thing) called "vacation." It was an experience. Now if you go buy a personal computer and spend $1,200, at least you have an asset that shows up on your balance sheet. The problems start when you're financing experiences and things on a long-term basis that don't have any long-term economic value, or when you are financing things where the interest that you pay far exceeds the value of the original asset. Experiences are good, just not good to finance.

The credit card has also allowed us to finance upward social mobility. Credit cards allow people to buy goods and services that their budgets cannot support. Our society's consumerist and materialistic (more stuff is better than less stuff!) culture began gaining momentum with the baby boomer generation. They wanted it all, and they wanted to keep up with the Joneses. Economist and sociologist Thorstein Veblen aptly identified this behavior to "buy things primarily for show" when he coined the term conspicuous consumption. With the credit card and new consumer attitudes, our society's value system shifted to where we define success through what we buy.

Credit also masks a lot of mistakes and it enables many bad habits. People want to find a fast and easy solution rather than address the source of the problem. When people feel sad or depressed they tend to engage in "retail therapy" which often results in a series of bad financial choices.[17]

As a society, we have been made to want things. We have taken wants and turned them into needs. This is easy to do when the credit card facilitates excessive spending. According to a financial literacy poll, the topic of credit card debt is a source of much denial for Americans.[18] People don't want to own up to the reality of their situations. Credit cards have allowed us to live today and pay tomorrow, or later, or never.

The result is a mountain of debt. The Federal Reserve Bank of Richmond reported that consumer debt began to rise significantly in the 1980s with increased credit card usage and credit's newfound use—home equity lines of credit.[19] They reported the following: "By 2000, household debt had grown to more than 90 percent of disposable personal income, and by the end of 2007, it had peaked at 129 percent." All this spending can't go on indefinitely. Or can it?

Data released Tuesday by the Federal Reserve Bank of New York show that at $11.52 trillion, overall consumer debt is higher than it has been since 2011. And more unsettling, debt is rising at rapid levels. Americans' debt—that includes mortgages, auto loans, student loans and credit card debt—increased by 2.1%, or $241 billion in the last three months of 2013, the greatest margin of increase since the third quarter of 2007, shortly before the U.S. spiraled into recession.

One analyst said, "We've already forgotten 2008 and 2009, and now we're projecting into the indefinite future and we're spending based on as if it had already happened." [20]

A culture bent on consumption, and the means to consume through credit, has clearly hurt Americans' personal finances. But why are all these bad decisions made in the first place? Don't we know better than this? The problem exists, largely, because financial literacy education fell through the cracks at home. Dual income or single parent households put children in the care of babysitters, daycare, and ultimately our public education system, none of which were prepared to take on the role of teaching personal finance. Most schools are focused on purely academic matters: math, science, social studies, and language arts. If financial topics are taught at all in schools, they usually appear in bits and pieces rather than as cohesive units of learning. In states that require focused financial literacy education, "64% of kindergarten through 12th-grade teachers reported feeling 'not well qualified' to teach those standards."[21] How can teachers teach something they do not know? Before we can teach financial concepts to our youth, we must first educate the teachers themselves!

If schools aren't teaching kids about how to keep a budget, the basics of credit, money protection, and growth, that duty falls back on the parents. But they're not doing it, even though studies have shown that it's parents who play the most important role in kids' mastery of financial literacy.[22] The time parents do have with their kids ends up being "compensation" for missed rearing (i.e. we spoiled them). Our time is fragmented, our lives move at a frenetic pace, and quality time often takes a back seat to the mantra of efficiency. Rather than acting as parents, we act as their friend. The mix of guilt, exhaustion, and tested patience puts parents in a situation where children can leverage the relationship to get what they want. On top of that is the sentiment among many parents, beginning with the baby boomer generation, that they don't want their kids to struggle financially like they did. This is a big mistake. Without a little struggle, people don't understand the value of a dollar. They don't learn what it means to be resourceful and self-reliant. Struggling and working through difficult situations allows people to stop, think, ask questions, and proceed with caution. It teaches people how to make the most of each dollar and make purchase decisions that are more prudent.

Financial literacy skills are important, but instruction on these topics is coming up short. The topics are inherently complex and often difficult to convey succinctly, but Acceleron Learning has designed a curriculum that overcomes these hurdles. We offer two products to close the gap on financial illiteracy. Accelerator Curriculum includes over 40 video lectures for adults and grades K–12 on topics such as financial foundations, financial instruments, and personal budgeting. Lifestyle Budget is a powerful set of planning tools designed to move you from theory to application. It helps students understand the financial implications of career and lifestyle decisions, and helps adults organize their personal finances and consider the financial impact of major life decisions. We'll discuss each of these products in detail in Chapter 8.

CHAPTER 5

Career Ineffectiveness

Self-Examination Question
What career challenges could you have
avoided with the right skills early on?

acceleronlearning.com

WHAT DO YOU want to be when you grow up? The first step is to know who you are professionally. This includes understanding your strengths, natural abilities, likes and dislikes, and how all these pieces fit together to form your personal brand and mission. The next step is to establish a written career plan. This starts with gathering the knowledge and skills necessary for career effectiveness, both technical and soft skills. Then you have to find and land a good job. As many people have discovered during the recent economic downturn, job hunting can be a complicated and exhausting process. Those fortunate enough to secure good jobs must develop a knack for handling interpersonal interactions with tact, and work effectively and efficiently. It is not enough to simply have the right degree and good grades. Surprise—you have to actually perform! People must also think about how to advance professionally and continue to acquire new skills to stay relevant. As a superpower economy, surely we do this well, right?

Nope. We're unhappy at work and don't know what to do about it. Yet, so much of our individual and cultural identity is placed on our careers. Is this to a fault? Probably so, but career satisfaction and clarity are still vital because we spend much of our time at work. Satisfaction increases the odds of financial stability and allows a person to make the most of their natural talents and abilities. The big philosophical questions concerning work are: what is the purpose of work, and does work need to be personally fulfilling? Some say *work should be fulfilling in and of itself*, while others suppose that *work doesn't have to be enjoyable: it is simply a means to an end—a paycheck, and to enjoy time off from work on weekends, holidays, and vacations.* Those who subscribe to the paycheck mentality are often checked out. Can you really live for the weekend, as the 1980s pop song claims? Is that really *living*?

Being content in your professional life also has health benefits. Studies show a link between career effectiveness and a person's physical and psychological health. Gallup's work showed that people who are more engaged in their work are happier, enjoy weekdays just as much as weekends, and have lower cholesterol and triglyceride levels. Researchers concluded that career effectiveness may very well be the most important aspect of a person's overall wellbeing.[1]

However, many people just don't like their jobs, or don't know what kind of work they would really like to do. Researchers for Gallup's *Wellbeing Finder* asked participants if they like what they do every day [for work], and only 20% responded with a firm yes.[2] This statistic is depressing, especially for people who have the capacity to improve their situation but don't do anything about it or don't know how to enact change.

Why are people so frustrated and disengaged? It's a combination of poor job fit, disillusionment with the realities of work, and a lack of preparation to deal with the workplace effectively. Parents and educators do little to help young people identify passions and career paths and distinguish between the two. This distinction is important, because passions and career paths are not necessarily the same thing. Passions can be hobbies, but your career needs to pay the bills (don't forget that fact!). Parents tell kids to follow their dreams and do whatever their heart desires. Children often go through K–12 and college with uninformed hopes and dreams. Once they graduate and enter the working world, they are miffed because it's nothing like what they expected. Work is hard, and oftentimes, the dollars don't line up with the dream.

Do you know enough about a career path to pursue it effectively? Many students change majors several times throughout college. That is, if they go to college at all. Suppose you put 100 students, all sophomores in high school, into a funnel. How many would come out the other end having achieved the college success vision consisting of a degree in hand, properly employed in their field of study, making a livable salary? The picture on the next page may surprise you.

In an interview with MSNBC, Dr. Fritz Grupe said, "Eighty percent of college-bound students have yet to choose a major... Fifty percent of those who do declare a major, change majors— with many doing so two and three times during their college years."[3] Throughout college and after graduation, many students still don't have a clue what career path they really want to pursue. This is causing them to run out of money and time.

Undergraduate students are taking longer to complete bachelor degree programs that were designed to be completed in four years. A study found that less than 55% of first-time students at the average four-year college graduate within six years, and at many institutions students have less than a one in three chance of earning a degree—even as they spend thousands of dollars on tuition and accumulate thousands of dollars of debt.[4] It is shocking.

As a nation, we are not doing kids any favor by loaning out tens of thousands of dollars in student loans to "follow their dreams" without helping and guiding them through the process. For example, let's suppose that student X has taken out $50,000 in student loans, is about to enter year three of college, and is just beginning to work on his major. Uncertain of what direction he really wants to go professionally, he decides to take a semester off to "figure things out." Is this student likely to

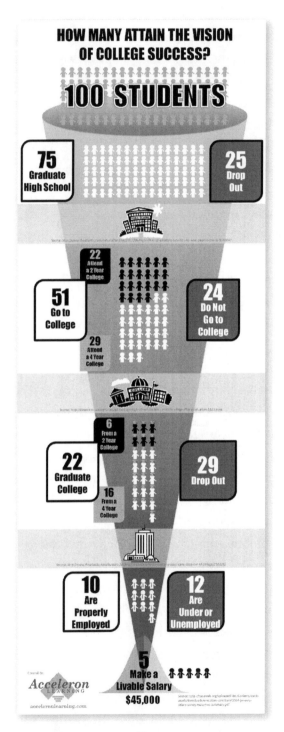

pay back the loans? Maybe not. In situations like these, lenders are basically giving away free money. Not only that, you're putting the taxpayer on the hook because the federal government backs about 84 percent of student loans.[6] The American Institutes for Research Report estimated that "Taxpayers have paid billions of dollars in subsidies to support these students as they pursue degrees they will never earn...dropouts cost the nation $4.5 billion in lost income, and lost federal and state income taxes."[7]

College tuition costs are rising faster than the rate of inflation, requiring students to take on even more student loan debt. From 1985 to 2011 the overall inflation rate increase was 115.06% while the cost of college tuition increased by 498.31% during that same timeframe.[8] The Goldwater Institute, a libertarian think tank, contends that "most of the growth in higher education costs come from administrative bloat, with administrative staff growing at more than twice the rate of instructional staff."[9] Student debt is taking up a larger portion of our nation's consumer debt. Debt from student loans is now greater than consumer auto loan or credit card debt and 53% of those with student debt don't believe they can pay it back.[10] Worse still, student loans do not expire and cannot be discharged in bankruptcy. People age 40 and older are responsible for nearly one-third of the nation's total student loan debt.[11] Many Americans in their sixties still have student loan debt. If they don't pay it off, their Social Security checks may be subject to garnishment.

One recent idea is to forgive students of their loan debt in a bankruptcy situation. If our nation allows bankruptcy as a remedy for unpaid student loans, we are essentially letting people walk away from their bad financial decisions. That's not fair to people who have made conscientious career plans and have paid off or are diligently paying off their school loans.

Private lenders and the federal government loaned out money in good faith to students. Parents, advisors, and educators may have played a role in a student's poor career planning, but students are ultimately responsible for the decisions they make. Condoning these bad financial decisions harkens back to entitlement. People believe they deserve a college education, even if they can't repay student loan debt. Student aid is not free money, but many people have begun to treat it that way.

An interesting phenomenon is happening. Currently our nation has a huge shortage of employable college graduates in many fields. But how can that be with all this unemployment? The answer is college graduates studied the wrong things based on job market demands. According to *U.S. News & World Report*, the top five jobs for 2014 that are expected to grow through 2022 are shown in the column to the left.[12] However, the most popular bachelor's degree programs are shown in the column to the right.[13]

	Top 5 Jobs	Top 5 Bachelor's Degrees
1	Software developer	Business administration
2	Computer systems analyst	Psychology
3	Dentist	Nursing
4	Nurse practitioner	Biology
5	Pharmacist	Education

Despite current labor trends pointing to an increased need for college graduates with medical, science, and technology degrees, many students continue to pursue degrees that are not in high demand. Nursing is the only popular bachelor's degree program that directly results in a marketable job for 2014–2022. While a biology degree may lead towards dentistry or pharmacology, the path is not direct. More startling is that the top two jobs, both related to computer science, are conspicuously absent from the list.

Does a student's education and career path position them for financial success? For many students the answer is no. Students are taking out thousands of dollars in student loans for liberal arts degrees that are not demanded in today's job market. A current labor market trend has young college grads working in low-paying jobs: "Young adults with bachelor's degrees are increasingly scraping by in lower-wage jobs—waiter or waitress, bartender, retail clerk or receptionist, for example—and that's confounding their hopes a degree would pay off despite higher tuition and mounting student loans."[14] Many college graduates find themselves in jobs that have nothing to do with their college education. The May 2011 Work Trends survey by the John J. Heldrich Center for Workforce Development at Rutgers University's found:

Just 44% of college graduates characterized their first job as "closely related" to their area of study, and a mere 27% characterized their first job as "a career." Only 52% felt that their college degree was necessary for their job, and 33% felt that they were working below their educational level.[15]

It is a huge slap in the face for grads to find out their college degrees are practically worthless in jobs where interpersonal skills, following directions, and basic computer skills are what is most needed. In fact, a 2013 study by Georgetown University found that "nearly 30% of Americans with associate's degrees now make more than those with bachelor's degrees. [Even though] by mid-career, many bachelor's degree recipients have caught up in earnings to community college grads, the other factor that has to be taken into account is that getting a four-year degree can be much more expensive than getting a two-year degree."[16] Students go through college expecting that they will find a high-paying job right after graduation, but they are still under-employed. In 2013 the Labor Department reported that "Americans under 25 make up a disproportionately large number of the unemployed relative to their share of the working population (16.4% vs. 10%). Many are staying in school to avoid the harsh job market. And those who are employed are working fewer hours and making less money than before the recession."[17]

This is really about basic supply and demand. The greater the supply is, the cheaper the labor. The job market has a high demand for college graduates with technical degrees, like science and health, and a low demand for liberal arts degrees.[18] This reality does not negate the intellectual and cultural value of liberal arts, just the economic realities of pursuing those fields of study. However, President Obama drew harsh criticism from academia when he insinuated that skilled manufacturing was a better career path than art history (which economically, it is). The resulting firestorm prompted a handwritten note from the President to acclaimed art history professor Ann Collins Johns:

Ann,

Let me apologize for my off-the-cuff remarks. I was making a point about the jobs market, not the value of art history. As it so happens, art history was one of my favorite subjects in high school...

...I was trying to encourage young people who may not be predisposed to a four year college experience to be open to technical training that can lead them to an honorable career.

Sincerely,
Barack Obama[19]

Among four year degrees, one occupation the current job market has a high demand for is petroleum engineers. In 2012 the median salary for a petroleum engineer was $130,280 per year, and all you need education-wise is a bachelor's degree.[20] A student pursuing a theatre degree from a four-year college wanting to work as an actor will have a different job outlook. In 2012, the median pay for actors was $20.26 per hour, which is $42,140 per year if you're lucky to get full-time work, and most people aren't that lucky.[21] What makes matters worse for the theatre student is you don't need a college degree to work as an actor, so many more people are qualified for that type of work.

To many, it is a baffling fact that job market trends dictate salary prices. If the demand is high for petroleum engineers, then the salary for petroleum engineers will also be high. If students pursue education paths that line up with what the job market demands, then the job market will eventually return to equilibrium. This means the underwater basket-weaving jobs that currently have very little market value and pay minimum wage will eventually become scarce. At that point the market demand—and salary—for those jobs will increase.

We are remiss in not explaining to young people that current marketplace trends have an impact on the college degree program they choose. Why aren't colleges sitting down with students on day one to discuss how different college plans will affect their lives post-graduation? The conversation might go something like this:

> "You want to major in music...mechanical engineering... education? Well, here are the financial implications, career path, employability, starting salary, lifestyle, and this is the upper end of your career trajectory. Now is this what you want to do? If yes, then sign up right here. If you don't want that, let's find something else for you to do."

You may be surprised to learn that most colleges *don't have that conversation* with students because they might lose business. The last thing academia wants is to tell a student that the degree he or she is pursuing has no marketability and that the student stands little chance of paying back his or her student loans. Even as the U.S. Education Department and legislators work to provide college-to-employment outcomes, NAICU, a lobbying group for 963 private, nonprofit schools opposes the push for data transparency, saying "There is no proof in it that the school you went to and what you majored in is the cause of your salary."[22] That is intellectually dishonest and deeply opposed to the primary reason that students in America go to college—to improve their career and salary prospects. Further, college admission materials often tout how much schools care about student success, but a no-holds barred article in *The Atlantic* neatly dispels this notion:

"The entire multibillion-dollar, 2,000-campus American college system—with its armies of salaried professors, administrators, librarians, bursars, secretaries, admissions officers, alumni liaisons, development-office workers, coaches, groundskeepers, janitors, maintenance workers, psychologists, nurses, trainers, technology-support staffers, residence-life personnel, cafeteria workers, diversity-compliance officers, the whole shebang—depends overwhelmingly for its very existence on one resource: an ever-renewing supply of fee-paying undergraduates.

It could never attract hundreds of thousands of them each year—many of them woefully unprepared for the experience, a staggering number (some 40 percent) destined never to get a degree, more than 60 percent of them saddled with student loans that they very well may carry with them to their deathbeds—if the experience were not accurately marketed as a blast. They show up on campus lugging enormous Bed Bath & Beyond bags crammed with "essentials," and with new laptop computers, on which they will surf Facebook and Tumblr while some coot down at the lectern bangs on about Maslow's hierarchy and tries to make his PowerPoint slides appear right side up. Many of these consumer goods have been purchased with money from the very student loans that will haunt them for so long, but no matter: it's college; any cost can be justified. The kids arrive eager to hurl themselves upon the pasta bars and the climbing walls, to splash into the 12-person Jacuzzis and lounge around the outdoor fire pits, all of which have been constructed in a blatant effort to woo them away from competitors…

And every moment of the experience is sweetened by the general understanding that with each kegger and rager, each lazy afternoon spent snoozing on the quad (a forgotten highlighter slowly drying out on the open pages of Introduction to Economics, a Coke Zero sweating beside it), they are actively engaged in the most significant act of self-improvement available to an American young person: college![23]

The common argument is that the information exists. The student just needs to ask for it. That's the equivalent of a parent saying *"If my kid would have asked if it was okay to play in traffic, I would have told him no."*

Parents and educators need to stop telling kids to pursue their passion without assuring kids are informed of and understand the economic consequences of the decision. It is inconceivable to think a university takes tuition money from parents and students, knowing full well the major and job the student is pursuing will pay little above minimum wage. Passions can coexist as a hobby for a while, but you need a career that will enable you to pay your bills and have a financially viable future. To reiterate, it's not about killing a student's passion. They just need to be informed about the financial implications of their career path.

Many college grads struggling to find work in today's job market turn right back around and go to graduate school. The thought process is that an advanced degree will provide additional skills to differentiate you from other job-seekers. Do your homework because some advanced degrees payoff while others do not. Someone with a music or English undergraduate degree might say, *I wish I had known that I wasn't going to have a job coming out of school, and that I'd be waiting tables...I guess I need to go back and get a master's degree.* Perfect! Now you are going to get a master's degree in an unmarketable field, so you can be *really unemployed* and in even more debt. If you can't get a job in your field with a bachelor's degree, what makes you think having a higher degree in the same field will position you any better? Even if you decide to pursue an altogether different field, you may not have the prerequisite skillset to do so. Furthermore, a graduate degree is an investment decision. Can you earn more money with an advanced degree than without one? Before pursuing a graduate degree, students should understand whether or not the marketplace will reward the additional effort and expense.

In an article titled "Is a Graduate Degree Worth the Money?" Georgetown's Center on Education and the Workforce reported that the return on investment of getting an advanced degree can range anywhere from 1% to 190%.[24] Several factors impact the value of an advanced degree including wage differential, marketplace demands, market saturation, and which college you attended.[25]

While the economic and intellectual benefits of a college education are well documented, college is not necessarily *for everyone*. Those who are on the fence about college (due to ability, interest, or finances) often fail to seriously consider the possibility of attending vocational school for a career in trades. These degrees take less time and some trades even pay better than jobs requiring four-year college degrees. Why are vocational programs overlooked? Because getting a college degree has become a rite of passage. Not having one has become some sort of scarlet letter.

Compare an electrician with an accountant. These are two

jobs that have about the same earnings trajectory. After two years of training, testing, and licensing, an electrician's total net earnings is $53,025.[26] A financial reporting accountant makes about the same salary ($50,921) and must also go through testing and licensing as well. However, an accounting degree requires a four-year investment. And let's not forget that really great electricians can end up owning their own companies too. Do we need accountants? Of course, but people need to understand that college is not the only (or guaranteed) way to enhance your earnings potential or build career satisfaction.

Certifications for career enhancement are also overlooked. This underutilized career strategy can help to differentiate you from other job-seekers. Certifications provide practical knowledge in a specific field and show quick results. To sweeten the deal, employers may pay or reimburse employees for getting relevant certifications. Certifications and licensure "can provide job security, credibility, and increased earnings potential."[27] Certifications are available for a wide array of occupations, not just the science and technology sectors. It just takes research to find one that is relevant to your field and appealing to employers. For example, a civil engineer may consider the Construction Manager certification; a business professional may consider the Internet Meeting Professional certification or the Business Manager certification; and a teacher may consider getting certification in special education for gifted and talented children.[28] For a small investment of time and money, people can acquire advanced subject knowledge and credentialing that is valuable on the job and is highly attractive to employers. Certifications and licensure won't break the bank or require you to miss years of income while in school.

Just don't forget, making it out there requires more than a degree. Employers want soft skills. But, many students undervalue internships, focused extracurricular activities that build their personal brand and résumé, and demonstrated experience in their desired field. This is a huge oversight that results in an undifferentiated résumé. College grads may have the technical skills needed for a particular job, but they are sorely lacking in soft skills. Dr. Natalie Lundsteen, former MIT Assistant Director of Graduate Career Services, whose PhD focus at Oxford was on internships and student readiness for the workforce, said:

Students aren't prepared to be professionals. They might be numerate, they might know how to analyze or plug things into Excel, but they don't understand what's referred to as... applied skills: how to communicate, how to work in teams, how to keep your mouth shut, how to listen, [and] how to find a mentor.[29]

A GPA by itself is hollow without internships and activities that put your knowledge to work. Students need to experience the world of work before they enter it. They need to learn about the career or industry they will be working in and how their degree program prepares them for that. It's not a given that the person with the highest GPA lands the job. Employers are looking for candidates who are well-rounded individuals who have a balance of solid academic performance and relevant experience in their desired field.[30]

College internships allow students to simultaneously apply what they know and begin networking, both of which are critical components for getting a job today.[31] A high GPA alone may show potential employers your book smarts and that you did the work, but that isn't enough to differentiate you among the sea of new grads entering an unforgiving job market. A study showed that "students who had internships or work experiences related to their studies while in college also benefited, earning roughly 20% more than those who did not. Those doing an internship ($34,680) had a median income of $6,680 more than those not doing one ($28,000)."[32] The value of internships is supported by a National Association of Colleges and Employers survey that found students who did internships had a 38% better chance of getting a job after graduation.[33]

Pairing excellent grades with one or more internships gives college students a better chance of getting a well-paid job in their field after graduation. According to the Bureau of Labor Statistics, the job market is grim, with a 5:1 ratio of job seekers to job openings.[34] A study by the John J. Heldrich Center for Workforce Development at Rutgers University confirmed this dismal job market: "Only 49% of graduates from the classes of 2009 to 2011 had found a full-time job within a year of finishing school, compared with 73% for students who graduated in the three years prior."[35] Students need to start building their résumé with relevant activities and start looking for apprenticeships in the beginning of vocational school or internships their freshman year of college.

What about stepping into the workforce? Most college graduates do not know how to look for a job. The employability of new grads frustrates their difficult situation: "Fewer than half of employers—44%—plan to hire recent college grads in 2010," according to a CareerBuilder survey. That's about the same as last year but down from 58% in 2008 and 79% in 2007."[36]

Another report showed that about half—53%—of U.S. residents who earned a four-year degree between 2006 and 2010 were employed full time.[37] College graduates, many of whom either haven't prepared a resume or don't know how to create one, are ill-equipped to land a job. What many students don't realize is they should be spending time during college looking for jobs and networking with peers and employers in their field. Instead, many students begin the job search post-graduation without the skills to make it productive. They think they deserve a job and it will come to find them. That's just not the case.

Children have been taught from a young age that *everyone gets a trophy*. Children learn to believe they deserve something regardless of how much effort they put forth. Michael Brunner, CEO of Brunner advertising agency, remarked on a conversation he had with a friend:

> Recently a friend of mine told me he planned to take his two boys to play in a soccer tournament over the weekend.
> When I wished them luck, he said, thanks, but luck wasn't a factor. No team really loses, he noted. Everyone gets to play. In fact, everyone gets a trophy.

We are guaranteed to fail at something, eventually. Without experiencing failure in a "safe" environment (like the soccer field), it is more difficult to learn resilience. The labor market is not the soccer field. Some people get good jobs while others do not. The student who is proactive, engaged with his or her studies, work experiences, and extracurricular activities will likely be the one who lands a good job. The one who feels entitled will not. Brunner said:

The young professionals I see are smart, great at multitasking, and whizzes when it comes to technology. But there's something missing: Many lack interest in working hard and investing time in a career or an organization that doesn't consider their needs before all others... A new word I have started to hear in the workplace is "deserve," and I am beginning to hate it. "I think I deserve an opportunity to work on that account." "I feel I deserve the opportunity for an interview with your company." "I deserve more money." I see too many kids who enter the workforce and expect to win just by showing up.[38]

We don't deserve anything, and we're not special until we actually do something special. The author of the American Freshman Survey, which has surveyed millions of young adults, found that "college students are more likely than ever to call themselves gifted and driven to succeed, even though their test scores and time spent studying are decreasing" and that "the tendency towards narcissism in students is up 30% in the last 30-odd years."[39]

In addition to an entitlement mentality, many new employees come with baggage: personal problems spilling over into the workplace, personal debt, disorganized personal and professional lives, and sinking productivity. Many of the common courtesies, etiquette and good manners are not so common with today's younger generations. These flip-flop wearing, iPod donning, social media-driven twenty-year-olds have to be reminded of what is and isn't appropriate in the workplace.

For those who do enter the workforce successfully, they must contend with the realities of work. Things like motivating others, managing one's time, running a meeting or a project, managing conflict, defining and solving problems, presenting effectively, and making the most of workplace culture and work styles. Many employers remedy this by providing employees with on-the-job training, but this comes at a huge cost and lost efficiency. The cost to employers of training each new hire is $40,000.[40] Because on-the-job training is expensive, the prospect of hiring new graduates who are likely ill-equipped is less appealing to employers. They want employees who can do the work and solve their problems fast, and those employees are hard to come by.

Career decisions are critically important, but often are poorly handled. We need to help college students get out of school in four years. We need to help them lay out the courses and extracurricular activities that will build a great résumé. We need to help working professionals make smart decisions to navigate and advance their careers. As you'll see in Chapter 8, Acceleron Learning offers three products that are designed to close the gap on career ineffectiveness. Insights @Work profiles dozens of career fields and industries, and Degree Tracker helps students plan their entire college experience for on-time graduation and effective career launch. Then, Accelerator Curriculum provides over 70 video lectures for adults and grades K–12 on topics like building your brand, managing people, and managing work. Each of these products will be explored in greater detail.

CHAPTER 6

Legal Illiteracy

Self-Examination Question
What legal challenges could you have avoided with the right skills early on?

acceleronlearning.com

THE U.S. LEGAL SYSTEM is built on a strong ideological foundation. People are presumed innocent until proven guilty. In recent years, however, our society has become so litigious that annual cost of civil lawsuits to the U.S. economy is estimated at $233 billion dollars, or $809 per person.[1] We have gone from treating laws as instruments that protect to devices that destroy. Columnist George Will pointed out:

> Today's entitlement culture inculcates the idea that everyone is entitled to a life without danger, disappointment or aggravation...The land of the free and the home of the brave has become "a legal minefield" through which we timidly tiptoe lest we trigger a legal claim. What should be routine daily choices and interactions are fraught with legal risk. [Once upon a time], rights were defensive. They were to prevent government from doing things to you. Today, rights increasingly are offensive weapons wielded to inflict demands on other people, using state power for private aggrandizement.[2]

The U.S. legal system was not intended to act as a giant slot machine. It exists to assure fairness in legal proceedings. Frivolous lawsuits are not in short supply. How can we forget the McDonald's coffee spill lawsuit? So many lawsuits are due to a lack of personal care and attention. People abuse the legal system by blaming their own blunders on an innocent third party. A study found:

> ‣ Seventy-six percent of those surveyed feel that fear of frivolous lawsuits discourages people from performing normal activities.
>
> ‣ Only 16 percent trust the legal system to defend them against frivolous lawsuits.
>
> ‣ 67 percent strongly agree (and 27 percent somewhat agree) the tendency for people to threaten legal action when something goes wrong is on the rise.[3]

In light of these stats, we owe it to ourselves to understand how to navigate through the system and ensure that outcomes are as fair and equitable as possible. Legal literacy means having a basic vocabulary regarding legal processes and procedures. It's about knowing when to engage an attorney or legal expert. Legal literacy ensures the welfare and security of our citizens, and reminds us of our legal obligations to society.

Most people will eventually encounter a situation that requires an understanding of the law. Everyday events have the potential to result in legal action: a car accident, a prescription for the incorrect medication, an insurance policy that doesn't pay the promised benefits, a subcontractor hired to remodel your home who doesn't complete the work, or a teacher who abuses students. The list goes on. You may find yourself dealing with personal bankruptcy, settling an estate, confronting workplace issues such as wrongful termination and unfair discrimination, or maneuvering through common misdemeanors and felonies. Cases like these fill our courts. People who never expect to deal with legal action may very well face that reality. It can be unexpected and costly.

If you are married, the likelihood of encountering divorce

is 50/50, and it isn't cheap. The business of divorce is a hopping market. According to maritalstatus.com, the average legal expense associated with divorce is $20,000 which amounts to $28 billion each year.[4]

Misunderstandings and failure to follow through on contracts is a major area of legal concern. If you've ever signed a contract such as a lease, car loan, or mortgage, you know there is plenty of fine print. Consumers who don't take the time to read and understand the terms and conditions are furious when unexpected costs come their way. *That's not what I signed up for!* But, did they read the contract? Failed contractual agreements occur all the time. The roofer who was subcontracted to fix the hail damage does a shoddy job. Your credit card interest rate suddenly goes through the roof, and you're left with a payment you cannot afford. Why does this happen? Frankly, it is because people are ignorant of the mechanics of law and how it applies to the situations of everyday life. "I see many, many times employers who are angry at students who have signed a contract, or taken a signing bonus, and then a few months later decide 'Oh I really don't want to work for this company anymore,'" said Natalie Lundsteen.[5] People don't understand the contracts they sign or don't understand the legal ramifications of signing them.

The number of civil lawsuits filed in fiscal year (FY) 2010 was 282,895, a 2% increase from FY 2009.[6] Bankruptcy filings make up an even larger portion of cases filed:

In 2010, the U.S. bankruptcy courts received 1,596,355
bankruptcy petitions, a 14 percent increase over the number
received in 2009. This year's [2010] total was the highest since
2005, the last full year before the Bankruptcy Abuse
Prevention and Consumer Protection Act of 2005 took
effect.[7]

With debt from student loans reaching the $1 trillion
mark, outpacing consumer debt from credit cards and car
loans, and the push for legislation changes in the bankruptcy
code, this nation could see the number of bankruptcy filings
increase as students default on their loans.

Another growing area for lawsuits in the United States is
medical malpractice.[8] Physicians order more preventive
screening tests and procedures primarily to cover themselves
from the risk of medical malpractice lawsuits.[9] Many of these
tests are unwarranted, and sometimes even harmful to patients.[10] Insurance companies respond to higher claims by
raising the cost of coverage, so it is a self-perpetuating cycle.

Legal casualties are everywhere in the workplace. Poor
ethical decision making, white collar crimes, negligence, and
intellectual property right infringement are some of the more
common legal concerns. These lawsuits are splashed all over
the news. Companies like Enron, Worldcom, and ImClone have
become synonymous with legal crisis. The Federal Bureau of
Investigation and the Association of Certified Fraud Examiners
reported that white-collar crime carries an annual cost of $300
to $660 billion.[11] If you own a business, you are liable for pro-
ducing safe and effective products and services. You are liable
for fair advertising that doesn't misrepresent your products or
services, and doesn't unfairly discredit competitors. If you have

employees, you are liable for maintaining a safe working environment and staying in compliance with labor laws. Who is paying these costs? You and I! It is buried in the price of every product and service we purchase. Legal illiteracy is a problem that comes at a cost to individuals, small businesses, and large companies.

According to the U.S Bureau of Labor Statistics there were 728,200 lawyers employed in the United States in May 2012. And they all have to eat. With the abundance of lawyers, finding the right one can be difficult if you don't know what you're looking for. Choosing the first lawyer you search for online won't give you much insight into whether that lawyer can meet your legal needs within a budget you can afford. Making an uninformed decision is an expensive way to approach legal assistance. Not knowing basic legal concepts can lead people to take on unnecessary legal expenses.

Getting legal assistance isn't like buying a pair of jeans or deciding what you want to eat for dinner. It's an expensive and complex decision. According to Lawyers.com the cost of legal assistance is highly variable, ranging from $50 per hour on the low end to upwards of $1,000 on the high end, as costs depend on several factors including location, type of legal assistance needed, and whether the lawyer is a seasoned professional or fresh out of law school.[12] Compared to rural areas, legal fees in big cities are usually double the cost, between $200 and $400 per hour, because those law firms employ a large support staff of paralegals and legal secretaries.[13] What people may not realize is you're also paying for the support staff needed to keep the attorney's law firm running smoothly.

Because the cost of legal assistance is dependent on several variables, it is difficult to estimate the total cost. Total costs for a civil lawsuit can range from $25,000 to $50,000.[14] If you don't understand how legal fees add up, you could spend a lot more money than you need.

Despite the variety of legal situations, and the cost of resolution, legal literacy in the U.S. is a topic that doesn't get much attention. At the writing of this book, a simple Google search for the phrase "Legal Literacy" yielded virtually no results on scope or impact of the problem in our society. Yet, go have a simple conversation with friends about what constitutes a legally binding contract, or the legal steps involved in home ownership, and you'll quickly see just how little people understand. While primary and secondary education teaches basic political science and government, applied Legal Basics is skimmed over or not part of the curriculum.

People do not know how to handle legal transactions, respond appropriately to legal problems, or understand the severe implications of making uninformed legal decisions. To mitigate these shortcomings, Acceleron Learning has created over 35 video lectures for adults and grades K–12 on Legal Basics as part of Accelerator Curriculum. These video lectures cut through the legal lingo to offer straightforward explanations about common legal transactions, criminal and civil procedures, and workplace law. We'll explore the details in Chapter 8.

CHAPTER 7

Personal Illness

Self-Examination Question
What wellness challenges could you have
avoided with the right skills early on?

acceleronlearning.com

A NEW STATISTIC from the Centers for Disease Control shows that Americans are now living an average of 78.7 years.[1] Average life expectancies for Americans were 47.3 years in 1900, 68.2 years in 1950, 70.8 years in 1970, 75.4 in 1990, and 76.8 in 2000.[2] We are living longer, but are we healthier?

Each day, we are confronted with choices about proper diet and nutrition, getting enough exercise, dealing with medical issues, and taking steps to prevent illness. We are faced with difficult situations involving loved ones such as addictions and drug use, eating disorders, or mental illness. Our social fabric is knitted by the good and the bad. We confront bullies at school, deal with difficult coworkers, seek to build social networks, and engage with our community. All of these things make up personal wellness. Are you prepared to navigate this landscape?

Let's begin by looking at physical illness. Preventive cardiologist Dr. Suzanne Steinbaum warns that Americans' increased life expectancy should not be taken for more than that: "'With the increased incidence in obesity, diabetes, high blood pressure, high cholesterol, we're going to start seeing people getting sicker younger.'"[3] We may boast about longer life expectancies, but with that we also boast the highest obesity rate in the world.

We are confusing quality of life with quantity of life. People are content eating high-calorie foods devoid of healthful nutrition. People are not fazed by their neglect of exercise and sleep. Pills are available to remedy nearly every physical or emotional complaint. These attitudes and behaviors are increasing health care costs. People do not take personal responsibility for their health. They would rather have others (insurance companies and the government) pay for their poor decision-making. It is no wonder that health care reform is a source of much frustration and contention among Americans.

Good health starts with how you fuel your body. The typical American diet, however, is unhealthy. Poor diet choices set people up for sickness, disease, and ultimately, greater dependence on the healthcare system. John Mackey, co-CEO of Whole Foods Market, said:

> Many of our health care problems are self-inflicted with over 2/3 of Americans now overweight and 1/3 obese. Most of the diseases which are both killing us and making health care so expensive—heart disease, cancer, stroke, diabetes, and obesity, which account for about 70% of all health care spending, are mostly preventable through proper diet, exercise, not smoking, minimal or no alcohol consumption, and other healthy lifestyle choices.[4]

The average American diet consists of a massive 51% refined and processed foods, 42% dairy and animal foods, and a mere 7% of fruits and vegetables.[5] Poor eating habits begin in childhood. A survey of children aged 6–11 from 1977 to 2002 found that while consumption of vegetables decreased by 42%, consumption of several unhealthy food choices increased significantly: Pizza increased by 413%, salty snacks increased by 320%, candy increased by 180%.[6] Americans have a disastrous take on nutrition and eating a healthy well-balanced diet. It's a double whammy: Americans are eating more of the bad things and less of the good things. Even if we know that we are eating poorly, the numbers show we are doing very little about it.

It is not just our bodies that are harmed by bad eating habits; "to supersize has become an accepted verb."[7] Lexicon has an effect on how people view the world and define themselves. The cultural acceptance of words like supersize has the effect of lessening the problematic behavior behind it. In some countries, such as France, people pride themselves on maintaining trim physiques. This cultural ideal means portion sizes are smaller, and it is unacceptable to take second helpings. *To supersize* is not part of the cultural lexicon. The food that Americans supersize contain increasingly large amounts of the *use-sparingly food category*—sugar, salt, and added fats. These foods may have helped humankind survive in pre-agrarian times, so the desire to consume foods containing these is part of basic human nature. The food industry has exploited this to our detriment.[8] Fast food restaurants, convenience stores, and vending machines are only a few of the places where the food industry knows they have the upper-hand. A person who is hungry is more likely to make a spur of the moment bad food choice because untamed hunger becomes an urgent biological need that demands an immediate response—something that is often fast, easy, and chock-full of fats, sugar, and salt.

Another strike on the American health-o-meter is lack of exercise. The average American doesn't get nearly enough exercise. In the Gallup *Wellbeing Finder* study, researchers found that a mere 27% of Americans surveyed got the recommended amount of exercise: 30 minutes a day, five days a week.[9] Americans are eating too much of the wrong foods, eating less of the healthful foods, and not exercising. But this isn't really news to you, is it?

Epidemics such as cardiovascular disease and obesity are

on the rise in the United States. While some nations have obesity rates as low as 3–4%, the United States ranks as one of the worst at 33%.[10] Childhood obesity is accelerating at a fast pace. Estimates reported in 2007 showed that the percentage of obese children in the United States has increased more than three times the rates over the past 20 years.[11] Being overweight is a risk factor for obesity and cardiovascular disease. Statistics show that 63% of the American population is overweight.[12] Being overweight or obese also has economic consequences. According to *USA Today*, people who are overweight or obese cost the United States $270 billion each year.[13] These costs manifest as health care expenditures and missed work due to injury or illness.

Type II Diabetes, a disease which is mostly preventable or controllable with proper diet and enough exercise, is another indication of our nation's poor health. The Gallup Organization reported that people with Type II Diabetes who made just one change—a healthier diet—had decreased levels of glucose, triglycerides, and cholesterol, and they decreased their need to use prescription medication to control Diabetes symptoms by 43%.[14] Taking small steps toward living healthier lives has shown significant results for people struggling with disease.

Getting enough sleep is another commonly neglected habit. The value of sleep is unmatched. "Getting a good night's sleep is like hitting a reset button."[15] People need sufficient sleep to recover and prepare for the next day. Currently, people are getting an average of 6.7 hours on weeknights, causing a whole host of problems, including difficulty remembering things, a sleep-deprived appearance, irritability, and difficulty concentrating on tasks.[16]

Americans are in denial that it is their habits, not the

health care system, that are the biggest contributor to poor health and wellbeing. Everyone knows those bad habits have a cost, but it is astounding just how much those costs have risen. For example, health insurance for a family in 1999 was about $5,700; in 2009 that number was $13,000; by 2018 it's expected to reach $25,000.[17] Many people cannot afford their medical bills or the cost to insure themselves and their families. People often forgo health insurance entirely if they cannot afford it through the traditional market, and do not qualify for state-funded health insurance. When catastrophic health problems arise, people without insurance, or without adequate insurance, become inundated with debt. A 2007 Harvard study showed that "62% of all personal bankruptcies in the United States has [sic] [have] a medical cause."[18] Out-of-pocket health care costs send many people into unmanageable debt.

Many Americans want to take the easy way out when it comes to fighting illness. They don't want to put in the effort to exercise more, eat better, get more sleep, and manage stress. People just want a pill to miraculously solve all of their physical and emotional pains, and the pharmaceutical companies are happy to oblige. You see this with the abundance of diet pills, sleeping pills, energy pills, focus pills, and pain pills available. A study by the Centers for Disease Control revealed "enough narcotics are prescribed every year to medicate each and every adult in America every day for a month."[19] The prescription drug frenzy in the United States is simply covering up bad lifestyle choices and illnesses that are a result of those core problems. Instead of treating the source of our society's health problems, we treat the symptoms. Sometimes the pills people take create new health problems.

Another problem is mental illness, which unlike physical

illness receives less attention from mainstream media. It is a largely misunderstood and taboo topic of conversation. In movies, newspaper articles, and children's cartoons, mental illness is frequently portrayed through a very negative and pessimistic lens. Popular films like *A Beautiful Mind* portray mental illness through exceptional giftedness. In contrast, films such as *Shutter Island* portray people with mental illness as crazy, dangerous, and violent. These stereotypes perpetuate society's misunderstanding and hesitation to discuss such topics. This ultimately exacerbates stigmas and prevents people from seeking treatment for mental health problems.[20] Stigma is a powerful fear and contributing factor to the many cases of mental illness that go undiagnosed and therefore, untreated.

Statistics show that millions of Americans are affected by mental illness. Here are a few compelling statistics:

> ▸ One in four adults—approximately 57.7 million Americans—experiences a mental health disorder in a given year;
> ▸ In the United States, the annual economic, indirect cost of mental illness is estimated to be $79 billion. Most of that amount—approximately $63 billion—reflects loss of productivity as a result of illnesses;
> ▸ Suicide is the eleventh-leading cause of death in the United States and third-leading cause of death for people ages 10–24 years. More than 90 percent of those who die by suicide have a diagnosable mental disorder.[21]

Mental illness encompasses a range of behavioral and mood disorders such as depression, anxiety, and addiction.

Mental disorders and illnesses can be caused by several factors such as chemical imbalances, genetics, biological functioning, and social environment. Symptoms can range from mild to severely debilitating and vary from person to person.

It is not just a matter of taking care of our physical and mental health. How we foster and manage social interaction has a big impact on our quality of life. However, social wellbeing is generally not taught outright. Instead, it is a matter of gathering personal experience and deducing, implicitly, how to interact with those around us. But as we seek relational intimacy and depth in a Facebook world, are we really learning how to interact effectively with one another? Do you know how to foster deep personal relationships and weather the challenges of life with a healthy support network at your disposal? CNN contributor Sherry Turkle recently commented:

> We seem lonely but afraid of intimacy. Siri, the social network, digital assistants, all of these give the illusion of companionship without the demands of relationship. The path we are on seems fraught with paradox about the most important human matters...We don't much want to talk about these problems. But it's time to talk.[22]

The digital world reduces inhibitions for virtual interactions, but when it comes to in-person communication, many people are uncomfortable and lost. Basic conversation rules and etiquette have gone out the window. People don't know how to keep the flow of a conversation going. They interrupt others, don't make eye contact, or portray body language that deadens conversation or makes for awkward encounters. The result is a decreased quality of life because we are inherently social creatures.

Pulitzer Prize finalist Nicholas Carr searches for the roots of this problem in his book *The Shallows*. Carr "looks to neurological science to gauge the organic impact of computers, citing fascinating experiments that contrast the neural pathways built by reading books versus those forged by surfing the hypnotic Internet, where portals lead us on from one text, image, or video to another while we're being bombarded by messages, alerts, and feeds. This glimmering realm of interruption and distraction impedes the sort of comprehension and retention [that] 'deep reading' engenders."[23]

Educators are lamenting the shorting attention-span of students. But rather than push back on the growing problem, instructors have come to advocate an "edu-tainment" approach. Deep content is aggregated to a superficial level, and focused learning is increasingly sacrificed in the name of fun. It is dangerous to conflate education and entertainment, and there is a major philosophical difference between saying that learning "can" be fun and that it "should" be fun. We live in a complex world, and are faced with complicated, multifaceted decisions in our personal and professional lives. It is unrealistic to reduce a topic like investment asset classes or family relationship dynamics into a glitzy, two-minute sound bite. Contemporary culture has become, as Takashi Murakami calls it, superflat. It's visually stimulating, but lacks any real depth. We're presented with "an abundance of consumer choices and technological advancements but [are left with] empty happiness, a sort of cute, cuddly, naïve hell."[24] Perhaps the old saying is wrong. The devil is actually in the lack of details. Dr. Sandra Bond Chapman, a neurologist who has studied brain health for over 30 years, points out that we must exercise our ability to focus, analyze, and process information. Truly smart people are able to synthesize things together because they practice making connections between seemingly unrelated things.[25] Educators—take heed! Cowering to the attention-deficit problems that contribute to poor focus and engagement in the classroom will only make those problems worse. You have to push back. You have to demand focus from your students and practice that discipline daily.

By nature, most of the topics residing under the personal illness banner are things that make for difficult or embarrassing conversation. And how do most people deal with difficult things? Avoidance. Rather than systematically describe and discuss the pressing wellness issues of our society, we simply do not talk about them. After all, they're "personal" problems. One way to help people open up about these issues is through education. Acceleron Learning offers over 50 video lectures for adults and grades K–12 on topics in physical, mental, and social health. Once informed, individuals are less likely to feel alone in their issues, and will be better equipped to approach a physician, counselor, or trainer. The next chapter provides an in-depth look at Acceleron Learning's products.

CHAPTER 8

Life Experience.
Accelerated.

Self-Examination Question
Are you willing to accept our
solution as a starting place?

acceleronlearning.com

THE OPPORTUNITY for prosperity, success, and upward social mobility achieved through hard work has become the American Nightmare. We have all of the trappings of the good life, but we don't actually have it. What we have, instead, is a façade that crosses all socioeconomic boundaries. Behind the walls of orderly homes are people mired in debt, searching for career fulfillment, dealing with legal strife, and worn down by physical, mental, and social illness. Those with money may be worse off than everyone else. Money adds fuel to the fire and magnifies the impact of bad habits and decision-making.

We're in trouble. Tens of millions of Americans are living a sub-optimal quality of life because they never learned core skills in financial literacy, career dynamics, legal basics, and personal wellness. In the words of psychologist Abraham Maslow, we are not *self-actualized.* We may be technically proficient and have all the optimism in the world, but without the practical life skills, we are dead in the water. It is striking, therefore, that these things *can actually be taught* but have never been organized, bundled, and delivered systematically in a way that is both easy to consume and cost effective.

Our entire economy is structured around the idea of specialization. Basic economic theory states that someone who specializes in a certain subject matter will produce more and higher-quality output because they have honed their skills in a particular way. The problem is that we've gone too far with this approach. Very few people are generalists. But, the person with generalist skills can capitalize on their rarity. It is the engineer who also has excellent people skills. It is the articulate writer who can also keep a budget. It is the entrepreneur who successfully starts businesses and manages employees with poise. To gain the competitive edge in business and in the working world, you need to be a specialist and a generalist. You need to acquire practical life skills. These give you the ability to identify and respond rather than react like a deer in the headlights.

So, who is responsible for teaching this stuff? If parents can't teach practical life skills because they don't know the subjects, and academia cannot because of constraints, indifference, or misplaced priorities, it is up to private enterprise to step in. Another obstacle is structure. Core subjects like math or reading are taught using an inherent structure, but practical life skills have never been approached in this way.

For these reasons, we created Acceleron Learning. Our goal was to develop a product that answers the immediate social need for practical life skills education. We want people to be proactive about their personal finances, career direction, avoiding legal issues, and taking care of their health. The starting place for all of these is a basic understanding of the concepts and vocabulary.

One of the challenges we faced was defining the scope of "practical life skills." What has guided the selection of topics is the immediacy of impact and the synergy between them. Take marriage as an example. People seeking marriage will encounter financial, career, legal, and personal wellness considerations. The same is true of home ownership or career direction. Everyone encounters major inflection points in life, and we want to provide a starting place for thinking through those points. Acceleron Learning is like a survival guide for life in a first-world country. As a refresher, the four pillars we identified are as follows:

- **Financial Literacy:** How to manage, protect, and grow your money. Examples include investing, insurance, using credit, planning for retirement, personal budgeting, basic economic theory, and how major life decisions have a financial impact.
- **Career Dynamics:** How to manage people and work to get your career on track. Examples include motivating others, defining and solving problems, project planning, preparing for interviews, and building the perfect résumé. Also included are topics that help students navigate college and effectively launch their career.
- **Legal Basics:** How the legal system works and how it impacts your professional and personal life. Examples include intellectual property, employment law, contracts, estate planning, and the legal impact of major life decisions.
- **Personal Wellness:** How to enhance your physical, mental, and social health. Examples include emotional health, balanced nutrition, building healthy relationships, and making the most of exercise.

Once the topic areas were determined, the next question was "How should we deliver the content?" Live lectures have a personal touch and allow for Q & A, but are constraining because you can only reach a few people at a time and they are costly to deliver. On the other end of the spectrum, most people do not want to read a lengthy guide on how to build a budget or diagnose mental illness. Our market research showed that consumers wanted to learn these concepts on their own terms at an affordable price. How do you simultaneously achieve the goals of engagement, cost effectiveness, and on-demand responsiveness at the same time? You go online with engaging video lectures and powerful planning tools.

THE PRODUCTS

Our four interconnected products include **Accelerator Curriculum**, **Insights @Work**, **Lifestyle Budget**, and **Degree Tracker**. Throughout the development process, we listened to everyone involved, talked to victims of the system, and looked for common denominators. The product evolved from people's frustrations and experiences with the current system. Our development team consisted of about 50 talented people, all of who cared deeply about bringing practical life skills education to life. Without further ado, let's talk about the products in detail. Check out the chart at right for an overview.

Accelerator Curriculum is our primary means of teaching practical life skills. It consists of over 200 video lectures on topics in each of the four pillars. The premise is this: if an expert had 30 minutes to tell you the essentials on a topic, like personal budgeting or how to manage people, what would they say?

The curriculum was created by subject matter experts and practitioners in each discipline. That's over 2,000 hours of development from PhDs, MDs, CPAs, CFPs, MBAs, MLHRs, JDs, and the like. We sought experts who had both a high level of credentials and hands-on experience. It had to be the right mix of theory and application, or we would miss the mark. So much of the information out there is either too shallow to be of value or too academic/technical to be consumed. On the shallow side, the Internet is littered with hundreds of "content mill" websites that offer worthless advice

Acceleron LEARNING

Life Experience. *Accelerated.*

Learn more at:
acceleronlearning.com

Practical life skills for everyone, taught through four *e-learning* products:

Accelerator Curriculum	Insights @Work	Lifestyle Budget	Degree Tracker
Financial, Career, Legal, and Personal Wellness topics taught with engaging video lectures.	Career exploration through assessments, major-to-career maps, and audio interviews.	Personal budgeting, tailored to an individual's financial aspirations and reality.	College experience planning to help students own their degree, from day one to diploma.
• 200+ video topics for K-12 & adults, :30 minutes each • 1,500 pages of supplemental instruction materials like quizzes, activities, and cases	• :20 minute structured audio interviews on career fields and industries • Requirements, how to get hired/advance, work/life balance, and pros/cons • Interest, workplace culture, and personality tests • Map college majors to popular career fields	• Reality check: Simulate the financial impact of a career path and spending habits in a personal budget • Create a personal balance sheet and understand financial ratios • Understand the total cost of home ownership with an easy to use calculator	• Build mission, goals and your personal brand • Create and manage a budget for school • Plan and sequence courses & extracurricular activities to maximize your college investment • Build a compelling resume and manage career launch

Curriculum Pillars

Financial Literacy

Career Dynamics

Legal Basics

Personal Wellness

and how-tos that could have been written by a fifth grader. On the academic side, you have well-intended instructors and courses that offer deep theoretical training without making appropriate real-world connections. Eventually, we found a formula that works.

Developed by subject-matter experts, each lecture is delivered by a broadcast professional and employs between 15–25 eye-catching presentation slides. Lectures are divided into two bite-sized segments for learning at your own pace, and are structured as follows:

> - **Concept Overview** – Summary of key points;
> - **So What?** – Why the topic matters;
> - **Concept Details** – In-depth information, tools, and examples; and
> - **Now What?** – How to put it into action.

For adults, we have about 120 lectures that are each 30 minutes in length. For grades K–9, we took the adult content (which can be used for grades 10–12 as well) and condensed it into age-appropriate concepts for the following groups: grades 7–9, grades 4–6, grades 1–3, and kindergarten. For these grades we have about 100 video lectures. A complete curriculum listing (as of the book's printing) is found in the appendix.

Everything about the K–12 lectures is designed to reflect the learning capacity of the audience. Slides contain less information and more images as the audience gets younger, the length of the lectures reduces to 10 minutes (each in two :05 segments for easier consumption), and the lecturers themselves are age-appropriate. High school students deliver content to middle school students, and middle school students deliver content to elementary students.

Additionally, each video lecture unit for adults and students is complemented by a robust set of age-appropriate supplemental materials that can be used for enhanced classroom or individual instruction. While quizzes are available online to all users, the rest of the materials either require purchase of the bundled product or in the case of the grey boxes, require the user to be part of an academic institution or organization. Take a look at the chart on page 92.

The online document repository contains around 1,000 pages of supplemental materials. Meanwhile, the instructor's guide contains over 500 pages of preparatory material, and the accompany student workbook includes 250 pages of discussion questions and activities for the video lectures and planning tools.

With dozens of lectures in each pillar, it can be a daunting task to "get into" the curriculum. So, we've created several ways to navigate through it. For starters, topics are sequenced into a logical order within each pillar. Next, we provide a curriculum sequence based on answers to commonly asked questions, like "How do I advance my career?" or "What do I need to know about home ownership?" We also offer an assessment tool where you answer about 30 questions that are designed to gauge your level of interest in subtopic areas. Then, the tool creates a custom curriculum sequence based on your responses. Finally, for institutional users **Accelerator Curriculum** can be used as a stand-alone course with recommended sequencing for high school, college, and organizational users based on time constraints and desired pillars of focus. As you can see in the chart, we include an instructor's

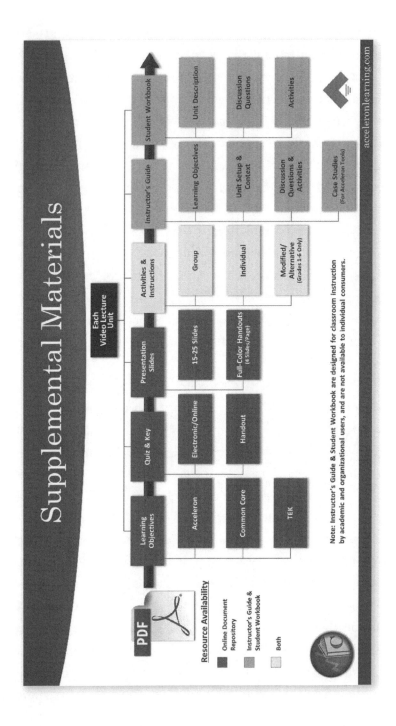

preparation guide, discussion questions/answers, and activities for each adult video lecture unit, and learning objective alignment and activities for K–12 units. Institutions can also create custom certifications, providing a "custom bundle" of topics to learners. As students pass quizzes associated with the certification, they earn credit towards completion. We believe that it is never too early or too late to begin acquiring practical life skills, and the **Accelerator Curriculum** is thoroughly designed to help you achieve that end.

Next, **Insights @Work** helps you understand the realities of working in a career field or industry. The modules include:

> ▸ **Personal Assessment:** Take a variety of assessments to understand your career interests, workplace cultural fit, and personality.
>
> ▸ **Major Exploration:** Explore how popular college degrees map to careers, and discover trade groups and job postings in your desired field.
>
> ▸ **Career & Industry Interviews:** Listen to over 150 broadcast-quality audio interviews using a structured set of questions, each 15–20 minutes in length, with career and industry professionals.
>
> ▸ **Career Roadmap:** Manage the end-to-end process for career and college planning. This detailed roadmap sequences a variety of Acceleron Learning content to help you make the most of your talents, abilities, and education.

You begin by taking an assessment to identify possible career paths. Once a few career options are identified, you should next understand how college majors map to those career fields. For example, an art history major might ultimately work in a museum, or in art sales/auctions, or creative design. After this bridge between theory and application is identified, you can then listen to interviews with people who are actually working in those fields or industries for practical insights. People frequently make life-altering decisions about pursuing careers in a particular field with partial information or unrealistic expectations. There's nothing like talking to someone who's "been there and done that." However, even if someone is savvy enough to have a conversation, they may not know what questions to ask or how to extract good information.

We're well aware of existing career resources on the market like *Wetfeet* or *Vault Guides*. However, these focus on providing a summary view, and we wanted to offer an "on the ground" perspective: something you would get by sitting down for lunch with a professional and conducting an informational interview.

We developed a structured set of questions so that responses would be consistent and organized. For career fields this includes 18 questions that profile the role, describe getting hired, advancing, and the nitty-gritty pros and cons of working in the field. For industries, we asked 16 questions that offer a profile of the industry, viable career paths within it, the structural economics at play, and trends that will impact the state and direction of the industry in the near term.

Then we sought dozens of professionals and conducted 15- to 20-minute telephone interviews. These interviews were produced like a radio call-in interview, and made to be easily consumed on our website or through our app. We also map each interview to several detailed career profiles from the Bureau of Labor Statistics Occupational Outlook Handbook. These profiles are updated regularly, and include a wealth of information that substantiates the insights offered by our interviewees. As with all of our products, the goal is to provide a well-thought-out starting place for the discussion.

Lifestyle Budget is an approach to personal budgeting that is tailored to your situation and spending habits. If you had $100 dollars to spend on anything, you might spend it on concert tickets, while someone else might buy a new outfit. In the same way, everyone makes different choices about how to spend and save money. **Lifestyle Budget** contains powerful tools designed for students and working professionals. It will help you take control of your financial situation, based on where you (want to) work, what you (want to) do for a living, the financial impact of major life decisions, and a reality check on the true cost of your financial lifestyle.

Regardless of your age, financial stewardship is a cornerstone of stability and success in American life. These tools offer a step-by-step approach to understanding money management, and to help you assess potential (or real) economic shortfalls. Recall the analogy about letting your kid play in traffic. A person who is uninformed about the financial implications of their career path, spending habits, or major financial decisions is going to get hit by a bus. These tools are designed (once again) to help you be proactive instead of reactive, and model different scenarios without the real-life penalty of failure. If you're already in trouble, the tools provide an approach and lots of tips for safely crossing the street.

Lifestyle Budget includes ten 30-minute video lectures that describe underlying concepts and help bring the tools to life. Details on each of the four modules are outlined on the following page.

▸ **Student Lifestyle Budget:** Create a budget that matches financial expectations with reality. First, you'll select from over 400 jobs to determine your starting salary. Then, select your location to determine tax and cost-of-living adjustments. Next, we'll help you assess spending habits in 16 categories, like rent, food, and entertainment through pre-defined, common levels of expenditure. At the end, the monthly budget summary helps you analyze spending and arrive at a balanced budget that works for your lifestyle.

▸ **Professional Lifestyle Budget:** A structured approach to collecting, inputting, and analyzing the factors that impact your real-world financial situation. You'll learn how to address budget shortfalls, manage expenses, and stay on track. Step-by-step, you can document your saving and spending habits in 14 categories. At the end, the monthly budget summary helps you analyze spending and arrive at a balanced budget that works for your lifestyle.

▸ **Balance Sheet Creator:** Step-by-step, we help you inventory your assets (what you have) and liabilities (what you owe), then automatically calculate your personal net worth (what you own). You'll also learn about common financial ratios that banks, creditors, and others use to assess your financial health including debt to income ratio, liquidity ratio, savings ratio, and debt to equity ratio.

▸ **Home Calculator:** Make nine simple inputs, and get an immediate assessment of the costs associated with home ownership. You can also see how your current housing costs align with expected costs. You'll get a custom report that details monthly house payment, insurance, maintenance, property taxes, utilities, association fees (if applicable), finish out costs, cash needed for down payment, and cash needed for closing.

Degree Tracker is a powerful suite of tools designed to help students plan and manage their education. The graduation rate at many American universities is abysmal. The primary reason for this is a lack of proper planning, ownership, and accountability by students. While colleges provide academic advisors for coursework and career counselors for résumé-building, the fact is that most students are not proactive. Students are not properly equipped to think through all of the moving pieces and optimize their college experience to graduate on time and on budget, with a résumé and a plan for finding a job.

We've talked to many academic institutions about the problem, and the common response is "Of course we help kids figure out their degree program and get through college!" Involvement is often more about administration than true career guidance. Furthermore, many colleges don't really have the resources required to impact their entire student population. Just imagine if 100, 1,000, or 15,000 students decided to get proactive and suddenly showed up at a school's advisement or career services office. The system would be overwhelmed. **Degree Tracker** pushes the decision-making and much of the accountability back onto the consumer (students and parents), rather than having it all rest with the academic institution. It is an empowered, self-guided process that takes away the intimidation factor and increases the odds of student success by creating ownership and accountability.

Degree Tracker has four modules to address all aspects of getting a college degree and launching into a career. Each module provides step-by-step instructions and tools to capture lots of information along the way. This information will help academic and career advisors (or parents) frame their conversations with students. The built-in reports also offer a status-check on an individual's progress. Degree Tracker includes ten 30-minute video lectures that describe underlying concepts and help bring the tools to life. Details on each of the four modules are outlined below.

▸ **Brand Builder:** Create a personal mission and brand statements to describe yourself, shape your career's direction, and attain your goals. We also provide the Brand Status Tracker, which shows the timing and sequencing of activities needed to build your personal brand as you work through school.

▸ **Budget Planner:** Almost half of college students who do not graduate in four years or drop out attribute their plight to financial problems. Budget Planner provides the structure to help you avoid this. See where your money comes from and where it goes, and make necessary adjustments to steer clear of money problems.

▸ **Path Planner:** Plan courses and extra-curricular activities in a timeline, plus capture details to build a résumé from scratch. Smart planning helps a student graduate on time and on budget, with a great résumé.

▸ **Career Launcher:** An organized approach to the job search process, from finding opportunities to applying, interviewing, assessing and comparing offers, and accepting a position. Manage the status and progress of each potential employment relationship and make "apples to apples" comparisons between offers and opportunities.

PRODUCT SYNERGY

By now, you're probably thinking—"Whew, that's a lot to wrap my brain around!"—and you're correct. But that is actually one of the product's strengths.

One way to look at Acceleron Learning is as a resource. No one expects that you'll read an encyclopedia cover-to-cover (or more accurately, webpage-to-webpage). Rather, it's designed to help answer a specific question at a point in time. Acceleron Learning can be used as a life skills reference in much the same way, which helps bring it to a manageable size.

Alternatively, we (or you!) can bundle specific content together, in interesting ways, to answer "big" questions like "What is the end-to-end process for developing a career plan?" Our answer to that particular question is a bundle of content called the Career Roadmap. We're including this roadmap (and a brief explanation) over the next few pages for two reasons.

First, it provides a structured approach to a question that thousands of students and parents routinely struggle to answer. As we've already discussed, the college/career decision is a costly one, and the steps to navigate into, through, and out of college are poorly articulated by most schools. This means that individual students are left to figure things out, often at the cost of additional student debt and a great deal of frustration. Second, the Career Roadmap illustrates how educators can create synergy across Acceleron Learning product components, and we hope it will spark creative problem solving with our content to answer other "big" questions.

Check out the Career Roadmap picture on the next page. While this illustration is linear (step-by step in one direction), a student should iterate (circle back) on each group of steps up to a particular "Yield" sign to arrive at the best decision. However, once you progress through a given "Yield" sign, it is more difficult to go backwards because of the decisions you'll make at that juncture. Here is an overview of each step, with the complete resource located as a tool within **Insights @Work**:

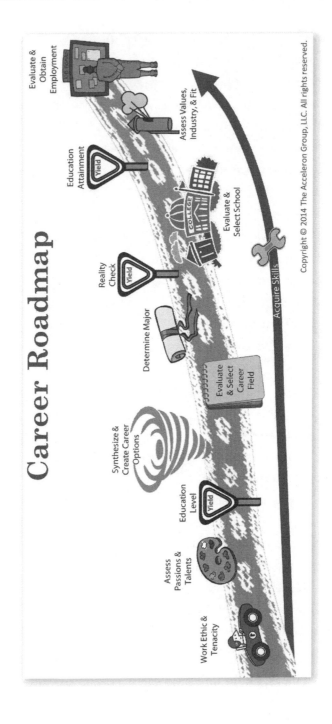

1. **Work Ethic & Tenacity:** What does it take to achieve career success? First, you must have a clear understanding of where you are headed. Then you must develop the grit, determination, and personal responsibility that will propel you towards your goals. This step teaches you how to develop such traits and write compelling mission statements/goals to frame your overall plan.
    Product Intersections: Accelerator Curriculum video lectures and Degree Tracker Brand Builder module.

2. **Assess Passions & Talents:** What do you enjoy doing (your passions) and what are you good at doing (your talents)? This step helps you assess and document personal and career passions, hard skills like math/science/reading/social studies etc., and soft skills for which you have particular understanding.
    Product Intersections: Insights @Work Assessments and review of Accelerator Curriculum topics to determine personal strengths.

3. **Education Level:** The level of education you attain (e.g. high school diploma through Ph.D.) has a direct relationship to the types of careers that will be available. Remember to think long-term! Your education and training should prepare you for a lifetime of career options, not just those available right after graduation. This step is the first "Yield" sign along the Career Roadmap, meaning that the decision you make here will have a major impact on subsequent steps. Everything you've documented up to this point should factor into your thinking about desired education level.
    Product Intersections: Insights @Work Assessments.

4. **Synthesize & Create Career Options:** How do you effectively combine your passions, talents, and education into a VIABLE career path? This step requires some creativity! For example, let's suppose your personal hobby is working on cars, you're interested in music, and you're good a physics. How might all of those threads be synthesized? Well, you could become an audio engineer for an automobile manufacturer! **Product Intersections:** Insights @Work Assessments.

5. **Evaluate & Select Career Field:** After identifying career options, you should conduct in-depth research to determine a specific career field to pursue. This step outlines the research process. **Product Intersections:** Insights @Work Career Field audio podcasts.

6. **Determine Major:** You next need to figure out the specific education requirements of your desired career field. What majors align to the field? Are there any professional associations you should research or join? This step helps you narrow the field of education options. **Product Intersections:** Insights @Work Major Exploration module.

7. **Reality Check:** Are your desired career field and major going to give you the financial lifestyle that you desire? It's a good idea to check BEFORE beginning additional education so that you don't take on unnecessary student debt! This step will help you simulate those implications and think about your overall short and long-term satisfaction level with the selected path. This step is the second "Yield" sign along the Career Roadmap, meaning that the decision you make here

will have a major impact on subsequent steps.
Product Intersections: Lifestyle Budget Student Budget module.

8. **Evaluate & Select School:** Several factors will impact where you obtain additional education. The goal is to optimize these items so that you increase the likelihood of graduating on time, on budget, and with a well-rounded resume. This step helps you think through those considerations.
Product Intersections: Accelerator Curriculum video lectures.

9. **Education Attainment:** Getting in is only the beginning. This step helps you create a financial plan to pay for school and make sure that your course work/extra-curricular activities are effectively building your resume and personal brand. This step is the third and final "Yield" sign along the Career Roadmap. How you manage this step will greatly impact your ultimate level of student debt, time in school, and career trajectory.
Product Intersections: Degree Tracker Brand Builder, Budget Planner, and Path Planner modules.

10. **Assess Values, Industry, & Fit:** Before looking at specific employers or companies, you should understand what you value in the workplace, the industries in which your skillset is useful, and where you may have the best overall fit.
Product Intersections: Insights @Work Assessments and Industry Sector Interviews.

11. **Evaluate & Obtain Employment:** In many ways, the job search process is like the college admissions process:

You have to decide what is important to you and narrow your list of prospective employers to a handful of viable options. This step will help you navigate the entire search process to land a great first job out of school.
Product Intersections: Degree Tracker Career Launcher module.

12. **Acquire Skills:** Throughout the Career Roadmap, you'll want to acquire both hard skills (technical, your degree) and soft skills (everything else!) to enable career success. This step helps you inventory those skills and make use of Acceleron Learning content to round-out your skill set along the way.
    Product Intersections: Degree Tracker Career Launcher module.

Beyond the Career Roadmap itself, the take away here is that all of these concepts are interrelated. As the folks at Gallup observed in Wellbeing: The Five Essential Elements, poor career choices have financial implications. Financial incompetence has legal consequences. Personal wellness is impacted by stability in the other three areas. For example, let's say you really don't enjoy the work you do. Over time, this may take a physical toll, making you sick because of stress. If you lash out at work in frustration, you could lose your job, which may put you at financial risk. If you hurt someone in the process, you could face legal consequences.

We believe that using our products will make you more perceptive of your surroundings, of how you process information, and of how topics in each of the four pillars relate to one another. Knowledge accumulates around the structures you already have in place. If you have spotty foundational knowledge in an area, it is much more difficult to learn new things and commit them to memory. Our products help you build and reinforce your "knowledge lattice" to make better life decisions. If a person spent 60 hours watching every video lecture we offer (for adults), they would walk away with a massive amount of practical life skills awareness, a library of methods for problem-solving, and a clear understanding of when to seek expert counsel. A person who used all of our tools would undoubtedly be better equipped to navigate through the complex decisions facing every high school and college student in America.

However, even small amounts of knowledge can have a big impact. It is the financially hesitant spouse who is empowered to research, finance, and purchase her first car on her own. It is the college student who finally understands how to combine his passion for music with his love of math to pursue a marketable degree in acoustic engineering. It is the fifth grader who can hold an intelligent conversation with his parents about bullying at his elementary school. These are all real outcomes from users of Acceleron Learning. Practical life skills are about improving everyday life for yourself and the people you care most about.

Our products are easy to use and cost under $99 for multiple years of individual consumer access, depending on the package selected. Institutional customers like colleges and organizations may be eligible for significant discounts based on volume. If desired, students can purchase the product just like a textbook, at no cost to the institution itself. Learners will have an immediately-useful toolkit of methodologies and approaches to address everyday challenges in each of the learning pillars. Instructors will get robust supplemental materials including discussion questions, individual and group activities, case studies, quizzes, and approaches to curriculum design. As a result, students will be aware and prepared to make smart decisions, and are also less likely to get taken advantage of by others. Our message is this: You don't have to learn the hard way. The stakes are too high and the school of hard knocks will knock you out. To reiterate, we believe that Acceleron Learning will enable you to:

> Understand foundational principles in each of the four pillars;
> Have a basic vocabulary in these subjects and be able to ask intelligent questions;
> Know when and how to seek professional advice on important life decisions; and
> Make higher quality decisions in life, with greater confidence.

CHAPTER 9

Mia Culpa

Self-Examination Question
Do you have the ability to enact
positive change in a big way?

acceleronlearning.com

ACCELERON LEARNING exists to offer practical life skills education at scale, for a low price. But we need you—a decision maker who is positioned to enact positive change—to get it into the hands of your employees, students, or family members. Broadly speaking, Acceleron Learning serves three market segments: education, organizations, and the public sector. Our products can be positioned as a resource for on-demand individual consumption, as a professional development product, as an HR benefit to employees and their families, as supplemental classroom instruction, or as a free-standing course. The chart on the next page offers a summary view of the markets that Acceleron Learning serves.

If our dissection of the issues with each pillar was not enough to fan the flames, we will now turn our attention to some of the ways that each of the major markets are preventing positive change from occurring. Parents, students, educators, politicians, and employers—many of you need a compelling reason to get into gear.

Why don't we head back to that dinner party you were hosting. Your guests were in a heated debate over who is responsible for teaching practical life skills. Just as the blame-game reached its crescendo, your practical life skills coach—we'll call her Mia Culpa—shows up at the party. She's got some words of "tough love" for each of your guests, and all of them are hoping she'll pin the blame on someone else. Let's see what she has to say to each.

The Markets We Serve

Education	Organization	Public
K-12	Wellbeing Benefit	Property Mgt. & Communities
Trade & Technical	New Hire Readiness	Social & Correctional Services
Higher Education	Professional Development	Churches & Affinity Groups
Individual Consumers	Cross-Cultural Readiness	Public Service & Military

Details on each sub-market listed above are at

acceleronlearning.com

acceleronlearning.com

Your Sister: *Why didn't anyone teach me this stuff?!*

Mia Culpa: You are the product of an imperfect system where teachers think parents are conveying practical life skills, and parents think K–12 education or colleges are doing it. In fact, nobody is doing it! Meanwhile, employers and society at-large expect you to know how to function with these skills in place.

We will talk about academia in a bit, so let's talk about your parents. For the sake of conversation, let's say that they did the best job they could in raising you. Several constraints may have prevented them from teaching you practical life skills. First, parents often find themselves in teaching moments unexpectedly. This requires them to provide an impromptu answer which may not be fully baked. Teaching life lessons as they come up can be helpful in the moment, but it is a scattershot method that lacks structure. Whole swaths of information can be missed because the questions were never asked in the first place.

Next, parents themselves may be unequipped to teach some of these things to you. Maybe they have gaps in their knowledge of the material, a lack of experience, or no access to good teaching tools. Another common problem? Embarrassment. Sometimes, parents may know the "right answer" but still make bad decisions. They feel like a bad role model. For example, if your parents are in the midst of bankruptcy, do you think they want to talk with you about good personal finance habits? Probably not. Same thing goes with career dynamics, legal basics, and personal wellness. We all have deficiencies, and generally do not like discussing those things with others, especially our kids.

Your Dad: *What more do you want from me? I'm just trying to keep things together!*

Mia Culpa: Your kids are the most precious thing you have. Give them a fighting chance to deal with life's challenges by making a clear commitment to teach and learn practical life skills at home.

Let's start with you, Dad. Do you and your spouse know this stuff, and are you prepared to teach your kids the concepts? Before you brush the question aside, just stop and think for a moment. Are you sure? Or are you simply too proud or embarrassed to admit you might need some help, too? If you're willing to take the steps for your kids, you should invest in yourself as well.

But let's say that you do feel equipped. It can still be tough teaching them. It's overwhelming and difficult to wrap your brain around. But Acceleron Learning is trying to change all of that with Accelerator Curriculum.

So make it a family mandate. The basic foundations are established early in life and built upon. As a parent, you lead by example (never forget that fact!). Set aside time to learn practical life skills together, and then strive to live them out. But, it takes commitment! In our busy and demanding lives, finding quality time to spend together as a family has become increasingly difficult. In fact, a study from the Annenberg Center for the Digital Future at the University of Southern California showed that of the Americans interviewed in 2008, 28% said they have less family time together, compared to 11% of interviewees who expressed that in 2006.[1]

How many hours are you spending with your family each week? In the early 2000s family time was about 26 hours each month, but by 2008 that was cut down to 18 hours.[2] In fact, an old saying puts it succinctly: *A family who prays together stays together.* For religious and non-religious folks alike, this adage can be applied to learning as well. Find time to learn together as a family. It can be fun and rewarding for all family members, and it is a good venue to open up discussions on everyday life. Discussions on practical life skills can set the stage for effective communication within your family. As the Gallup Organization denoted in *Wellbeing: The Five Essential Elements*, we often underestimate the impact of our closest relationships and social connections on our wellbeing.[3]

Your Sister: *Well that's a start for families with younger kids, but how is it that I'm half way through college and still don't know what I'm going to do with my life?*

Mia Culpa: Sadly, a lot of this goes back to your parents. Here's some hard advice for them: when helping your kids figure out what they want to do for a living, stop telling them to just *do what makes you happy.* This is setting them up for failure, unless they understand the implications of the decision. I'm not trying to kill dreams, passions, and ambitions. All of those things are important and give life direction and focus. The problem is that kids don't see both sides of the story. They are shown the sentimental side of a career path, but they often miss the details on the effort, sacrifice, time, money, and perseverance that are required to get there. They don't understand the success or failure rate, nor do they comprehend the impacts of their decisions.

You want kids to make an informed decision. They need to understand that it's always a good idea to have a Plan B if Plan

A doesn't work. At some point, your kids will have to support themselves financially. Parents: you do want them off your payroll eventually, don't you? Don't confuse a career choice with a passion. Passions, interests, and skills need to be aligned to marketable professions and clear expectations. Be realistic and be smart.

Your Dad: *So what should I do to help my kids succeed now?*

Mia Culpa: The best way to convey to kids the implications of a career decision—what job you want and how much that job pays—is by driving them around in a neighborhood that can support the hourly rate of the job they want to have.

Load up the car and point out neighborhoods that support a $10/hour job, $30/hour job, and so on. Let them know, *if you want to live in a particular kind of neighborhood, then this is what your hourly rate needs to be, and these are the professions that are going to earn it.* This is a very visual and tangible representation that you can share with your kids. Acceleron Learning's Lifestyle Budget effectively does the same thing, except in a highly structured way.

Then, you need to have due diligence regarding your child's career path before they go to college. This can't be emphasized enough. Did you know that 80% of students change their major at least once throughout college?[4] That means just 20% of high school graduates enter college with clear career direction. A study by the National Association of Colleges and Employers (NACE) revealed the many reasons, good and bad, for how students choose their major:

Sixty-six percent of students choose their major based on a career in which they are interested, 12% say they "drifted" into a major, 9% say they were inspired by a particular teacher or professor, 7% chose a major based on earning potential, and 6% say they were influenced by friends and family.[5]

Parents, do your kids a favor and remind them that they don't need to follow in your career footsteps. They need to find a career that maximizes their inborn traits and abilities. And you need to help your kids find out as much information as they can before going down that road. Have your kids talk to people in the profession to learn about the pros and cons, as well as training, skills, and résumé-building experiences that will enable their success. Kids need to know that the working world is not as glamorous as TV and movies tend to portray. Some jobs are downright tough, and your kids need to be aware of all these aspects ahead of time. Acceleron Learning's Insights @ Work helps students navigate these considerations.

Once your kids are in college, don't make the mistake of assuming good grades are the only thing sought by a potential employer. Have you ever crammed for a test? If you're lucky and your short-term memory is sharp, you performed well on that test. But does that test grade truly represent what you know? No, it just shows that you have a good memory. Your GPA and standardized test scores are important, but you need something to back them up such as internships, work experience, and extracurricular activities that supplement your career path. These accomplishments show that you care about your future, and know how to put your technical skills to work.

You also need to make sure your kids have a solid approach to graduating on time and on budget. That not only includes laying out a roadmap for courses, but also a sensible budget, and an approach to gathering experiences that build a great résumé. Then they need to understand how to search for jobs and make informed tradeoffs between different job opportunities. Degree Tracker does just that.

Your High School Teacher: *You said you were going to talk about academia. What role does K–12 education have in all of this? We're stretched thin as it is.*

Mia Culpa: This is not a matter of adding more stuff on top of your existing requirements. It's about incorporating practical life skills education into what you're already doing. For example, it could be incorporated in the classroom as complementary instruction, as a resource available to students, or as a free-standing course. Accelerator Curriculum includes learning objectives and classroom/individual activities designed to facilitate the Common Core State Standards used in about 45 of 50 states, TEKS in Texas, and financial literacy legislative mandates nationwide. To be clear, our product does not "teach to the standards." It only provides intersection points for educators to efficiently incorporate practical life skills into the classroom. Our desire is to make Acceleron Learning more consumable in public education, not to endorse or advocate any particular set of standards.

For the K–12 market, Accelerator Curriculum is integrated to teach practical life skills concepts in a building-block fashion for all grade groups. When the included supplemental materials are used, Acceleron Learning is a comprehensive drag-and-drop approach to lesson plan creation. Students and their parents can access the products at home to promote learning and engage family involvement outside of the classroom. Now we're talking paradigm shift. Your school is enabling the broader community to learn practical life skills and advocating continuing education. That builds goodwill and allows schools to give back to their constituents.

What about the cost? Before you raise budget concerns as an issue, here are a few things to think about. The U.S. Census Bureau reported the average public education cost per student per year was $10,499 in fiscal year 2009.[6] Virtually none of this money is allocated to practical life skills education, but recall the Michigan State University study where 80% of a person's success depends on it. Just like math, science, reading, and writing are required in all levels of education, practical life skills needs to be too. And really, it's not about spending a ton of money because, frankly, the total amount of money allocated per student had no correlation to performance standards set by the No Child Left Behind Act.[7]

Acceleron Learning can provide practical life skills for as little as $6 per student per year for individual student/limited at home access, and under $2.50 for classroom only access. It's a pretty inexpensive way to fill a major skill gap. An added bonus: school districts can completely offset the cost of the product by engaging community sponsors. Acceleron Learning offers pre-lecture video advertisements and messaging. Think about it. In exchange for a few thousand dollars per year, local CPAs, doctors, attorneys, and major employers can underwrite each of the curriculum pillars and bring these skills into the classroom. For businesses in the community, it is nice to show support and advertise on signage at the football stadium or place a well-wishes advertisement in the yearbook. However, Acceleron offers an advertising and engagement opportunity with major community impact.

Your Mayor: *So that's how the community can get involved. But what does it have to do with city government?*

Mia Culpa: More than you might think. Let's go back to Gallup's *Wellbeing: The Five Essential Elements.* As part of their research, Gallup conducted call-out research with thousands of people in major U.S. cities and every congressional district in the nation. They categorized each community as "thriving," "struggling," or "suffering." They can tell you exactly how your community is doing in Career, Social, Financial, Physical, and Community wellbeing. It's powerful information for officials at every level of government to assess the health of their citizens. Now, you're aware. So what if your community is struggling or suffering in an area? The next step is education. That's where Acceleron Learning can help!

Don't think that education just falls into the hands of state education agencies or local school boards. Municipalities provide all kinds of education services, including community centers, continuing education programs through school districts, the library system, credit repair services, and counseling services. All of these platforms can leverage practical life skills e-learning. For example, your local library could offer Acceleron Learning to residents, or the city could work with the school district to set up evening workshops that combine Acceleron and the expertise of local professionals in each wellbeing area.

An even bolder approach is to put Acceleron Learning directly in the homes of residents as an innovative wellbeing project, and engage a variety of stakeholders like PTAs, the chamber of commerce, religious institutions, and the local media to make practical life skills a community initiative. Think that's far-fetched? Acceleron Learning is working on just such an initiative (more details later)!

Your Mayor: *That's a great concept, but what if we can't get tax dollars behind it?*

Mia Culpa: Then go to your economic development people and solicit community or local business sponsorships. A little bit of effort can go a long way, here. Many people give lip-service to the value of community, but then they turn around and keep to themselves. It is a self-perpetuating problem. So why not kill two birds with one stone? Create community engagement through Acceleron Learning, while simultaneously improving community wellbeing through practical life skills education. Gallup points out that participating in community outreach programs actually fosters community wellbeing. What's more, "Community Wellbeing is interconnected with, and builds directly on, the other four [wellbeing] elements." Engaging community sponsors, experts, and citizens has an interconnected, multiplicative effect.

Positive social change can also occur in community subgroups. Any clearly defined, inter-connected group—churches, military groups, civic organizations, and the like—can rally around and benefit from practical life skills education. Gallup notes that positive social change occurs in groups because "they draw on positive peer pressure, social support, and accountability to others. Experimental research suggests that creating sustainable change may be two or three times as likely to happen in the context of a group, company, or organization [than as an individual going it alone]."[8]

Your College Professor: *You said that colleges aren't teaching practical life skills. I beg to differ! Students learn soft skills in the classroom, we've got a great student life office to promote wellbeing, and career services gets them ready for the real world. What's the problem?*

Mia Culpa: Take a look at how your product is working in the marketplace. It is failing. You have lost sight of who your product and customer is. Harsh words, I know. But hear me out.

The Association of American Colleges and Universities published a study that found 87% of employers believe higher education is losing its edge in the global market, and 63% of employers report that college grads lack the needed skills for success.[9] Your customers are unhappy with the product.

Institutions are caught up in spending money on big building projects, athletics, and lots of other periphery. Because you are focused on your own needs—answering big research questions, and posturing to impress the academic community—your students have become a by-product. They are a second-, third-, or fourth-level goal. What's even worse is that your students are financing all of this, and they are not receiving meaningful benefit.

A recent CNN report revealed that "the problem with education isn't money—we spend plenty—but quality...Instead of figuring out how to make education pay future dividends, higher educational institutions are building better dorms with flat-screen TVs, movie theaters and tanning salons."[10] What has happened to your priorities? Much of college has become a 4+ year cruise ship experience for students. You have to attract them with fancy amenities so that the tuition dollars keep flowing. Besides, if you don't keep up with the schools in a student's consideration set (i.e. the Joneses), you'll lose tuition dollars!

People are beginning to notice. Easy access to student loans means your institution has a blank check to charge higher tuition. This has a formal name, the Bennett Hypothesis, proposed by William Bennett, President Reagan's secretary of education.[11] Recently, a joint study between Cellini and Goldin, economists from George Washington University and Harvard, respectively, tested the Bennett Hypothesis on 2,650 for-profit colleges in three states with similar programs and tuition; each school either offered financial aid or didn't, which provided a fair assessment.[12] Their findings showed "The schools that received aid charged roughly 75% more in tuition than the schools that didn't."[13] We all know tuition is constantly on the rise, but with this tuition hike did the quality of education increase? No, but the quality of stadiums and libraries improved. We're not talking pocket change here. It's billions of dollars invested in capital assets that educationally speaking are fluff. And when the ship runs aground, don't expect for there to be a robust secondary market for unused stadiums and student activity centers. In fact, the Delta Project, which is a nonprofit group that studies the sources and uses of funding in higher education found:

A surge in spending by universities on nonacademic areas such as recreation and other student services. The study found spending in student services at public research universities rose 20 percent from 1998 through 2008, compared with 10 percent for instruction.[14]

We read about colleges spending $15–$20 million on a rec-
reational center, or $200 million on a new stadium, yet the
question remains: is this the best use of funds when so many
real challenges are faced by both students and employers?
Colorado State University apparently thinks the answer is yes.
The Wall Street Journal reports, "Faced with declining state
funding, CSU is raising money to build a $246 million, 40,000-
seat football stadium on its Fort Collins campus. University
President Tony Frank says the new facility will help build a
winning football team while advancing one of the school's highest priorities: attracting more out-of-state students paying
higher tuition." Even if the school is able to build a winning
team with this boondoggle project, the results of a 2007 study
show that private donations spurred by athletic performance
"usually last only as long as the success and [the donations
themselves] tend to be concentrated in athletics."[15]

Are schools in the football business or the education business? Regardless of who is footing the bill or why the project is
being built, these aesthetic improvements are a misguided effort to attract tuition and donation dollars and gain favor with
students who are looking for a cushy deal. And don't tell me it
is because schools want to improve their rankings. Let's look at
the kinds of things that U.S. News and others use to create the
rankings:

The indicators we use to capture academic quality fall into a number of categories: assessment by administrators at peer institutions, retention of students, faculty resources, student selectivity, financial resources, alumni giving, and (for National Universities and National Liberal Arts Colleges) high school counselor ratings of colleges and "graduation rate performance."[16]

What's missing here is the student and employer's perspective on how the product performs in the marketplace. Essentially, schools are keeping score and spending money on a bunch of things that don't matter in the final analysis. Big-name schools like UT Austin or the University of North Carolina are the worst offenders, spending an average of $1,729 per student per year on nonacademic services.[17] For as little as $6 per student per year, a college can offer access to Acceleron Learning to a student and have a real impact on career readiness.

Your College Professor: *Regardless of spending or ranking games, I still think that we have our priorities straight on the academic side of the house.*

Mia Culpa: Oftentimes, no. Colleges do not proactively inform students, parents, and the public on which degree programs are most demanded in today's job market. You do not require students to understand the economic implications of their degree decisions. Why not tell the music major the truth? The job market doesn't have many good jobs for flute players, or sociology majors, or lots of other degrees. Are these fields of social and cultural value? Yes, but the inherent limits of the degree are not something a student needs to find out after

$29,000+ of student debt and no promise of a job. You know which degree programs and education tracks match the needs of the current job market, but you fail to systematically inform students. Many college administrators say, "Well, just ask for the information and we'll provide it!"

That's not good enough. You don't have to pull your wallet out. You don't have to drop out of college because you ran out of money. You don't have to deal with the life-long consequences of choosing the wrong major or career path. You don't experience any of that. You pass that on. By the time a student figures out that he or she made poor choices or has skill gaps, graduation is near, or it's too late. The last thing a student wants to do is jeopardize degree attainment by rocking the boat. Students cannot get a refund for the product that they bought from you—their education. You have a responsibility to inform. An 18-year-old kid is not savvy enough to ask.

The problem is that colleges do not win in the short-run by fully disclosing this information. However, in the long-run it is the right thing to do for our economy and for the welfare of your students. No one is really positioned to push back on this issue. Students and employers do not have substantial (or any) organized representation in higher education, and no close substitutes exist for what you provide. The problems of higher education can be summed up in a statement from economist Richard Vetter:

> Consumers typically have believed that no good substitutes exist [for college]—the only way a person can certify to potential employers that she/he is pretty bright, well educated, good at communicating, disciplined, etc., is by presenting a bachelor's degree diploma. College graduates

typically have these positive attributes more than others, so degrees serve as an important signaling device to employers, lowering the costs of learning about the traits of the applicant. Because of the lack of good substitutes, colleges face little outside competition and can raise prices more, given their quasi-monopoly status. (2012)

Now I'm not going to disagree that education is very important, and students that have the capacity for it should get it. The issue is that college education may not necessarily be for everyone, but you and your institution have created an "academic industrial complex" in the United States which is *everyone should go to college.* The Labor Department reported in 2010 that nearly half of working Americans with college degrees are in jobs for which they are overqualified. That's an oversupply of 13.1 million degree holders, and is one reason that "among retail sales clerks, 25% had a bachelor's degree in 2010. Less than 5% did in 1970."[18]

Visionaries, in search of an alternative to traditional college education, have begun to offer online college level courses for free. YouTube has also caught on with their EDU Portal, boasting over 22 billion views.[19] Another is Khan Academy, which provides several thousand education videos in a tutorial format, is getting four million unique hits each month.[20] Forward-thinking educators believe that tutorial style teaching, such as Khan Academy, is more effective than traditional methods, and will play a role in reforming this country's education system. These online courses provide the same information taught in your college classrooms, but they are reaching far more students who don't have access to college, cannot afford college, or who need an alternative learning environment. Even within the traditional academic framework, politicians like Texas Governor Rick Perry are pushing for a dramatic rethink of higher education, proposing accelerated or cut-rate $10,000 college degree offerings at state institutions.[21]

Acceleron Learning's products are not intended to threaten you or your institution. The products act as a complement to what already exists, and the concepts are presented from a practitioner's point of view, something that is often missing in academic environments. Here are a few implementation ideas: Acceleron Learning can be used during admissions to help students find their way through the initial maze of decisions around career paths and degree planning. As an onboarding tool, it shows students and parents that you care. It can also be incorporated into an orientation or freshman seminar course, or taught as a free-standing course during a student's academic career. As the online education landscape continues to develop, Acceleron Learning offers a certification process to help students express their soft-skills competency on a resume and differentiate from other applicants during the job interview process.

Do you understand the 80/20 statistic? Why do kids learn math? Because they have to, it's required! If practical life skills are treated like an elective, kids won't learn them. We don't need you to offer an elective on personal budgeting. We need you to force kids to learn it. Managing your money is not an elective activity in life. Within months of graduation, it is all too common for students to ask, "Why didn't anyone tell me how different the real world is from college? Why didn't any one teach me how to make it out here?" Sure, you teach some soft skills, and kids learn a lot through social interactions in college, but the approach is ad hoc. Academia bears some responsibility for this and Acceleron Learning is well positioned to help you bring a structured solution to the table. If parents are incapable of teaching these skills, you are perfectly positioned to take ownership of the situation and have a social obligation to do so. Put the money where it will truly impact the lives of your students and our society at large. Acceleron Learning's products help students make informed career decisions, build a plan, and learn how to make it in the real world.

Okay, so now a student has graduated and falls under the domain of alumni relations. Unfortunately, the last thing a new grad wants is to get a call asking for a donation. Students think, "Seriously, you've already gotten into my pocket for $50,000 or $100,000 and now you want me to give more money to you? So you can build a new stadium?" But that's exactly what happens!

Acceleron Learning can help here, too. One way you can make the donation process less insulting and more about establishing good *alumni relations* is by offering complimentary Acceleron Learning products to new grads during their first few years after graduation. This is a way you can show appreciation to grads for choosing your school. It also shows you care about their future by acknowledging that some big life decisions lie ahead. By creating goodwill with alumni, you have a stronger case for donations down the line. Your alumni will say, "Hey, my college really does care about me...at least they're doing something to benefit me rather than just trying to get into my pocketbook."

Your Boss: *So tell me, how do practical life skills actually impact the bottom line?*

Mia Culpa: The issues found in academia spill over into the workplace because you hire students, their product. New recruits face a steep learning curve when it comes to practical life skills. Facebook and flip-flops allowed at the office? I think not. Meanwhile, tenured staff is trying to deal with the personal fallout of their bad decisions, and prepare their children to face real-world challenges. What if you could address all of these symptoms at once? Acceleron Learning is designed to do just that.

You want your employees to do the work you hired them to do, right? The problem is that when an employee is stressed out about personal finances or dealing with wellness issues, those things carry into the workplace. In a Personal Finance Employee Education Foundation study, *Forbes* magazine reported that employees spend 15–20 hours per month dealing with personal financial problems while on the clock at work![22] If you're paying them $25/hour on average, that's $500 per month in lost productivity. Spending just a few dollars per month to educate employees and ease stressors will have a quick and lasting ROI. Remember, that doesn't even account for career, legal, and personal wellness time-drains in the workplace. If you see these problems and have the ability to enact positive change, then you should help your employees do something about it! At least, that's what Gallup believes:

> If you lead or manage people, your actions have a direct impact on the wellbeing of others. When leaders embrace the opportunity to improve employees' wellbeing, they create more engaging places to work and greater returns for the organization. And they even help strengthen their employees' families. But when leaders opt to ignore

employees' wellbeing—dismissing it as something that's "none of their business"—they erode the confidence of those who follow them and limit their organization's ability to grow.[23]

So you'll ultimately pay the price in decreased productivity, greater absenteeism, and higher turnover. A well-balanced person is a productive employee, and it's worth it to ensure that your employees' personal lives are in order. It actually improves your bottom line. Helping employees in their personal lives will also foster mutual respect. You show genuine care for employees and their families, and in return they arrive at work ready to do their jobs. *The Wellbeing* study found that employees who feel that their manager cares about them are more likely to be:

Top performers, produce higher quality work, are less likely to be sick, are less likely to change jobs, and are less likely to get injured on the job....[And] what's best for the employee isn't at odds with what's best for the organization.[24]

Someone who learns to make sound decisions in his or her personal life is going to make better decisions at work. If your employees are equipped, you're going to keep them around (the more problematic an employee is, the more likely you are to get rid of them). Know the value of a dollar and how to manage a personal budget? Odds are that you are going to make better decisions about stewarding company assets, too. Many of the soft skills, such as managing work, managing people, understanding the political and social framework of the work environment, are all part of Acceleron Learning's curriculum.

Okay, how specifically can your organization use Acceleron Learning? Offer the products as a human resources benefit for employees and their families. With adult and K–12 products, it can be used by your employee's spouse and children. Acceleron Learning truly is a benefit for everyone. It can be used on an individual basis, as part of your professional development program, as a free-standing training course, or as a resource on standby.

Being proactive in your employees' personal lives is a paradigm shift, and it will give you a competitive advantage. A small investment in your employees can yield big returns.

CHAPTER 10

Gaining Traction

Self-Examination Question
Do you have tenacity?

acceleronlearning.com

IN HER BREAKAWAY 1976 disco hit, Maxine Nightengale sang "It's alright and it's coming on, we gotta get right back to where we started from!"

At this point, more than 26,000 words into *Our Bad*, you probably want to know how things are going. Has the marketplace validated our hypothesis? Does the product actually work? As it turns out, Maxine is surprisingly instructive in answering these questions. We are definitely gaining traction, but in some ways *we're right back where we started from.*

One of the great ironies of our experience to date is that we have a product because existing structures (like K–12 or higher education) leave gaps that have historically gone unfilled. Acceleron Learning is designed to fill in the gaps and round out a person's education. The challenge is in finding a market with a strong appetite for filling those gaps. You see, if the existing structures truly understood the scope of the problem, we likely would not have had a product in the first place! This means that our hypothesis is correct—but also that we are not shielded from it.

To date, we have called on the career service offices, first year experience programs, and alumni relations offices at roughly 1,000 U.S. colleges. Despite the staggering research, the glaring need, and lack of coherent alternatives, our product has gotten a mixed reception. While feedback on the quality and scope of the product itself has been universally positive, the sticking point is always implementation. Here are some of the common reasons why that seems to be the case:

- ▸ "We already do that" – As our immense research indicates, a scattered, student-driven approach is not valid. However, this is the way that most colleges think about delivering practical life skill topics.
- ▸ "It's not our problem" – The job market would beg to differ, and it is naïve to think that colleges are not in the "employee creation" business (despite the internal focus on academic research).
- ▸ "We don't have the budget" – Colleges could if their priorities were straight. We're not talking about department-level budgets, but the misallocation of dollars to programs and projects across the institution.
- ▸ "We'll do it ourselves" – One school told us they had been working on developing an in-house solution for a decade, but nothing has yet materialized. Another said they thought that training all of the faculty members to teach these skills was better than using a 3rd party product. Let us know how that goes.
- ▸ "We'll get back to you" – No, they won't. Glacier-paced decision-making combined with zero follow-up equals the status quo.

The last item is by far the most common, as the following example illustrates. In 2013, we met with faculty and staff at a large public state university in Texas on several occasions. As the conversation progressed promisingly towards a sale, the associate provost for student success recommended that we conduct a focus group with students.

We met with half a dozen students for over an hour. We unpacked the concepts presented in *Our Bad* at a high level, demoed the product, then settled in for discussion and feedback. Reflecting back, the phrase that best describes the student reaction is "righteous indignation." Students were surprised at the scope of the problem, uninformed about the skills they were lacking, and very angry that no one at the institution had taken responsibility for teaching them those skills. In an effort to calm students, we assured them that their school's conversation with Acceleron was a positive indication of their understanding and willingness to help students. Immediately following the meeting, we received the following email:

> Ryan,
> We received positive feedback from our student group. Within the next several weeks, we hope to begin the search for a Experiential Learning Coordinator and would like for this individual to be involved in the decision to move forward with Accerleron (sic). I'll be in touch soon.
>
> Thanks again,
> (Name Withheld)

Despite multiple attempts to connect with them, we never heard from the school again. No follow up, no explanation, and no help for students. This pattern has repeated itself dozens of times, and I wanted to better understand why.

In the fall of 2013, I went inside the walls of academia by teaching a consumer behavior course at another large public university in the Dallas area. I used Acceleron Learning as a case-study to illustrate business and marketing concepts in the course, and solicited more direct feedback from students along the way. They read *Our Bad* and wrote reflection papers on how the concepts in the book apply to their lives. Here is a small sampling of responses from those college seniors:

> ▸ Reading *Our Bad* was a real eye opener. Not just
>   because it calls out what is wrong with our society,
>   but also because it actually made me look at my
>   own life and wonder what I am doing with it.
> ▸ I wish I would have read this book before I entered
>   college, to guide me and make better decisions with
>   my financial aid and the career path I have chosen.
> ▸ Before I read this book, I thought, "This stuff is all
>   common sense, what person doesn't already know
>   this?" I was wrong.
> ▸ I truly believe that the academic institutions are missing
>   the mark in terms of adding skill-building courses like
>   Acceleron to the curriculum.
> ▸ After much denial, I have realized that I too lack many
>   life skills that are very important once you are out of
>   school and in the "real world."
> ▸ In reading *Our Bad*, I feel both afraid of what the future
>   holds because I'm realizing I haven't been fully
>   equipped, yet hopeful because I see that there is a way
>   to figure everything out.
> ▸ After reading this book, my approach to life has
>   changed.

A mix of emotions follows these comments. On the positive side, the feedback is quite affirming of our vision and product. On the negative side, it illustrates just how urgent the need and gap actually are. The question, over and over, is "Who's really looking out for students, here?"

In addition to our formal discussion of Acceleron Learning in the classroom, I had many candid conversations with students who were seeking advice and guidance in their personal lives. One student, Richelle, came to me after class and said, "Here's the deal—I started college pursing marine biology, but realized that I didn't have the quantitative skills for the field, so I switched to business. Along the way, I discovered a passion for clothes and decided to major (within the business school) in fashion merchandising. Now I'm about to graduate and have no idea what to do with my life. Ideas?"

Hmm. Marine biology and fashion. After some consideration, I responded "Why not work as a buyer for a sporting goods company that focuses on water sports like SCUBA, surfing, and water skiing?" The light-bulb went on.

How many students are confronted with these kinds of situations? How many students have the foresight, like Richelle, to initiate the conversation? Aligning passion, talents, and economic viability is nothing more than an optimization problem, but so few students get the right kind of help to make their circumstances work together. Instead, they are passed through the system with very little push-back or critical thought. This hands-off approach is most evident in the rate of letter grade inflation in higher education over the last several decades. *The New York Times* reports:

> About 43 percent of all letter grades given were A's, an increase of 28 percentage points since 1960 and 12 percentage points since 1988. The distribution of B's has stayed relatively constant; the growing share of A's instead comes at the expense of a shrinking share of C's, D's and F's. In fact, only about 10 percent of grades awarded are D's and F's.
>
> The authors don't attribute steep grade inflation to higher-quality or harder-working students. In fact, one recent study found that students spend significantly less time studying today than they did in the past.[1]

At the beginning of the semester, I hoped to grade my senior-level students as an employer might "grade" a new employee's work product. However, the pressure to lower my expectations and inflate those grades quickly followed. On weekly in-class writing assignments, roughly one-third of students were unable to construct a coherent paragraph...and then there was the team project. The guidelines for this end-of-semester team project, comprising 25% of the course grade, were clearly described in the syllabus and discussed weekly in class. The project required students to produce a 15-slide presentation supported by about 30 research/back-up slides. On the due date, half of the project teams only submitted the 15 presentation slides with no supporting research. Half! Based on workplace standards, many of my students should have failed the class. However, I couldn't have actually graded this way because as a lowly new adjunct, the administration would have viewed me as being the problem rather than the students. It was not a battle I was prepared to fight.

It's easy to see how college profs are lulled into a "mail it in" mentality with teaching and grading when their primary success metric is research and publishing. But at least the research is adding value to society, right? Sadly, most of it is effectively worthless:

A study at the University of Indiana found that "as many as 50% of papers are never read by anyone other than their authors, referees and journal editors." That same study concluded that "some 90% of papers that have been published in academic journals are never cited." That is, nine out of 10 academic papers—which both often take

> years to research, compile, submit, and get published, and
> are a major component by which a scholar's output is
> measured—contribute little to the academic conversation...

There is no question that academic research, as a discipline, is important. The issue is, at what cost? Sadly, the esoteric focus of academia is most often at the expense of intentional student conversations and heightened expectations. The article goes on to say:

> ...Arguing that any study can be justified because we
> cannot know what research will prove useful is an un-
> falsifiable and unsatisfying reply to a current academic
> reality where research agendas must be monetarily
> prioritized. This "anything could be useful" approach is
> distinctly different from arguing that everything is useful.
> There must be some way to distinguish between the useful
> and the esoteric.[2]

My professorial experience brought to life many of the challenges articulated in our research. However, it would be unfair to lump all schools into this characterization, so let's highlight some of the places where Acceleron Learning is gaining real traction. Within higher education, our banner example to date is with The University of Dayton in Ohio. In the fall of 2013, UD began offering Acceleron Learning to freshman students majoring in business. Over the subsequent school year, we've received great feedback from students and begun working on a rollout approach to offer the product to all incoming business freshmen, including a "Soft Skills" certification program that will help students articulate their newfound capabilities in conversations with prospective employers. We're also talking with an online university consisting of more than 60,000 students and a major national business publication (which offers subscriptions to students) to offer Acceleron Learning as a value-add certification program.

Within K–12 education, we recently signed a major deal with a company called No Excuses University. NEU provides professional development and college readiness programming to over 6,500 teachers at nearly 200 public schools across America, reaching over 120,000 students. Teachers in the NEU network will receive access to Acceleron Learning for use in the classroom, as well as our latest feature, Connect, which brings everyone together with searchable user profiles, discussion forums organized around NEU topics, and a platform for sharing instructional and administrative resources. Through regularly scheduled webinars and the NEU conference series around the U.S., we'll be working with teachers to bring practical life skills to public education in a big way. A common thread with higher education and K–12 is that our product often works best when bundled with other offerings.

On the community engagement front, we're working with the Vandalia Butler City School District in Ohio to offer Acceleron Learning to all students and teachers in the school district, and to every household in the community. We're doing this as a way to move the needle on Gallup's *Wellbeing Index*, which puts Ohio in the bottom quartile for wellbeing in the United States.[3]

What's more, the school district will host community education events where subject matter experts can lend their perspective and engage individuals and families on these topics. The initiative will also involve local government, businesses, and religious institutions, uniting the community around a common purpose, practical life skill education! We expect Gallup and other national media to take notice of this innovative approach and are excited about the social policy conversations that will result.

Our little vehicle for practical life skills is roaring to life, heads are turning, and the wheels are gaining traction. Tenacity is the engine that makes those wheels turn.

CHAPTER 11

For Our Good

Self-Examination Question
Who comes to mind when you read
this book? Are you willing to help them?

acceleronlearning.com

IMAGINE WHAT MIGHT happen if large chunks of our population acquire even BASIC Financial Literacy. Rather than living beyond their means, being enslaved to debt, and falling victim to predatory practices by financial service companies, people might instead experience financial stability, or even financial freedom simply by understanding concepts in money management (budgeting), asset protection (insurance), and wealth accumulation (investing). Rather than avoiding the topic due to feelings of inadequacy or intimidation, people might begin to ask questions and engage in thoughtful conversation with their HR department, banker, or insurance agent. You know that 401(k) that you're dumping money into while it sits on autopilot? Or that health insurance policy you stuffed into a drawer because you don't understand it? Well, don't let other people who are either unscrupulous or indifferent dictate your financial wellbeing. Thoughtful conversations produce better results for you, the consumer.

Think about the impact of financial literacy on big life decisions like buying a home, getting married, or having a child. People will start doing the diligence and will make informed decisions, rather than simply trusting in the advice of the so-called "experts." On a macro-level, the impact is staggering. Informed consumers are scary to big banks, insurance companies, and financial advisory firms because they won't be taken advantage of any longer. Informed citizens are scary to complacent career politicians because their constituency will understand the financial impact of that upcoming local bond election, or those state spending decisions, or that big national policy debate. People won't let the wool be pulled over their eyes.

Consider how well-planned Career Dynamics will impact

our economy. At the core, people will be more likely to end up in jobs that they're suited for and that they enjoy. This means lower unemployment, greater productivity, and higher job satisfaction. On an individual level, folks won't spend tens of thousands of dollars on poor-fitting degrees or burn an extra one or two years in school, all the while racking up additional student loan debt and forgoing the income they would otherwise earn. They'll take some ownership of their career path and proactively pursue opportunities. Savvy employees make for savvy organizations. Rather than accept the marginal employees that are produced by many academic institutions, firms will begin to demand that the product meets the needs of the marketplace. The academic monolith will be forced to deliver or will be left behind as alternative education venues gain traction in the marketplace. Hmm, imagine that! With practical life skills on the career front, people will make better decisions on behalf of their employers and will be better stewards of company assets.

What if we are equipped with Legal Basics? For starters, individuals will make better decisions about the contracts that they enter into. This goes for all kinds of agreements, from mobile phone plans to mortgages, and better contracting means clearer expectations and outcomes for all parties. Individuals will begin to think about the legal implications of their actions when it comes to misdemeanors or felonies. People will be more thoughtful about matters of great legal consequence like estate planning or filing for bankruptcy. And in the workplace, people will pause and reflect when managing intellectual property or making decisions with ethical implications. People will understand what plagiarism is and why it should be avoided. Clarity about the people and processes of the law will result in greater steadfastness in the face of frivolous lawsuits or erroneous legal outcomes. The law will return to its core purpose—defending rights—rather than being hijacked as a weapon of ruin.

An emphasis on Personal Wellness will improve our collective physical, mental, and social health. People will begin to see the benefits of smart choices regarding nutrition and exercise. Individuals will be equipped to navigate through common issues like sleep deprivation or stress, and can approach social concerns like bullying or caring for an elderly parent with confidence. The net positive effect of maintaining a healthy physical environment, or engaging in healthy relationships, or volunteering, will enrich the lives of everyone in a community. On a large scale, we can begin to turn the tide on obesity and a litany of ailments like depression, addiction, or type II diabetes. A proactive population is one that is less dependent on medical treatment and is less reliant on pharmaceutical intervention. We can improve the very quality of our lives.

If you have a better grasp on practical life skills, you're going to make better decisions for yourself, better decisions at work, and better decisions at home. Ultimately, you are going to have a competitive advantage. Remember our discussion on the generalist and the specialist—successful people are both. Students with practical life skills are going to be more attractive job candidates. Employees with practical life skills are going to make smarter decisions at work and will be better positioned for advancement. The job market demands well-rounded, focused, and capable employees. Practical life skills will set you apart from the pack and give you that competitive advantage.

You're going to be more stable and productive, more efficient, and you're going to demand that from the public officials who represent you. Once they are held accountable this country may begin to turn around. If *we the people* continue to ignore these pressing social needs, the United States will continue to fall behind. Optimist, pessimist, or realist, the fact is that some very bad things are going on in our society right now. The economy is destabilized, stress and angst are very high on both sides of the political aisle, and the family unit—a building block of society—is crumbling. Practical life skills are a discrete contributing factor that must be addressed. You have the power to do great things with just a little effort, and that effort is called learning. This is about awareness and education.

Together, we can provide foundational knowledge and equip people with the right vocabulary to ask thoughtful questions and seek help when they need it. We can improve decision-making and help people begin to take ownership of their finances, careers, legal situations, and their health.

How can you start the discussion in your own sphere of influence? Remember that it takes both structural change and personal responsibility. Make this an agenda item at home, at school, at work, and in your community. Talk with your family about the issues and reflect on your own life. Identify the areas within each pillar where you need some help. Remember Hugh Dunno's story? Attend city government and school board meetings, and ask the tough questions. Hold officials to task, and demand a real plan to address practical life skills. If you are taking your child to visit colleges, be sure you ask specific, pointed questions about how they are going to prepare students to succeed in the real world. That's what you're paying for. At work, tell your HR department about Gallup's *Wellbeing* study and see how your organization is addressing the gaps. BUT—don't just talk about it. What matters is where we go from here.

There's no excuse for not taking action, either with Acceleron Learning or on your own. Just do something, and continue to challenge individuals, public and higher education, leadership in organizations, and our elected officials to take action on practical life skills education. Acceleron Learning is a starting place. It is ready to go, and it is extremely affordable. We want you to check it out and then tell us how to make it better. That's the goal: to make things better.

Now you know about *Our Bad*, America. Let's work together to provide access to practical life skills. It's for *Our Good.*

About Us

acceleronlearning.com

M Y DAD AND I are entrepreneurs. We wrote this book to get people thinking about practical life skills and the consequences of not having them. *Our Bad* is about the symptoms, causes, and implications of what's going on right now in our society, and how Acceleron Learning can help enact positive change. Much of who I am today (middle class values and entrepreneurship) is a result of how I was raised, which is a result of how my parents were raised. In particular: save money, do well in school, work hard, stay out of trouble, and take care of your body. Sounds a lot like the four pillars, doesn't it?

Much of my dad, Gregg's, background and upbringing contributed to Acceleron Learning's development. His father and mother only went to school until the 6th and 10th grades, respectively, but they understood the two kinds of knowledge are technical skills—learned at school, and common sense— how to think through things smartly. My grandparents taught my dad a lot of common sense (so it can be taught!) by discussing the potential consequences of his actions before he got himself into trouble. It was about being aware and being proactive.

My dad went to the University of Dayton. Thanks to an inspiring professor, John Rapp, Dad found his niche in economics and business. To this day, he says that John is his hero. After graduating in 1976 with a MBA, he went to work for General Motors, and got married to Mom—all within four months. Whew!

My parents moved from Ohio to El Paso, Texas in 1979. GM brought my dad and a few other guys down to Mexico to run their Juarez plant. In 1984, he left on good terms and through a series of entrepreneurial ventures, ended up addressing a key market need in Mexico, metal finishing. For nearly 20 years, my dad and his team acted as a dedicated, single source supplier to Ford Motor Company, having invented some pretty cool technology that hasn't yet been duplicated in the automotive industry.

After running the metal finishing business for a few years, he decided to fire himself and come back on as a consultant. My dad figured that if he could detach himself and just give sound advice, he would be more useful to his organization. Working as a consultant allowed him to have a lot more free time, so he helped people work through their life and business challenges. He adopted businesses at random and spent anywhere from three months to a year helping them free of charge. He also helped his friends and their families. What he found was a consistent need for practical life skills. By also mentoring at-risk kids, he realized that if you are going to make a difference in someone's life, you should start early and focus on root causes.

The first big entrepreneurial project we took on together involved NASCAR. In 2004 my dad and his best friend Tom Georges hatched a crazy scheme. As avid NASCAR fans they wanted to put an El Paso, Texas-themed car in the Sprint Cup Brickyard 400. The goal was to make it a community initiative, and bring positive national media exposure to our border community. I had just gotten home from Baylor for the summer—it was mid-May—and Dad proposed that we put a car in the Brickyard, which was August 8. That was akin to putting together a football team for the Superbowl in three months. But we thought, sure, why not?

So we engaged local businesses and raised $100,000 from them in exchange for advertising space on the car. We put together a team, got the El Paso Convention and Visitor's Bureau behind us, revved up the local media, and went for it. Along the way, we donated all net proceeds of the effort to a Fort Bliss Fund designed to help children who had lost a parent in the Iraq war. We took the car to the Brickyard 400 in Indianapolis. It was fast, but engine trouble kept us out of the race. This was a hard lesson in the highs and lows of entrepreneurship. It taught me how to dream big, work hard, spend wisely, give back, and deal with failure gracefully.

Even though we had failed, we had still accomplished a lot. We went from sitting in our living room to the race track in the course of a summer. We got local businesses and community leaders involved and did something positive for the community. And we did it on a super-tight budget. The average per-race budget for a team is about $400,000. We showed up for less than $100,000.

After some thoughtful consideration, we decided to give racing another run in 2006. This time my dad financed the car out of his own pocket. We included all of the sponsors from the first car, for free, and unveiled a new "Sun, Salsa, Smiles" car design for the people of El Paso. We also set up a fund for the El Paso Diabetes Association to help promote healthy living. Through fundraising we were able to install a complete gym at their facilities for use by area children who are affected by the disease. With Chad Chaffin behind the wheel, we made it into the 2006 Brickyard 400 and finished the race. With exposure from the Associated Press, across cable television, and on NBC during the race, it was a big success from El Paso's perspective. It highlighted our community's spirit and sense of adventure.

Other than being a cool story, why does this matter? When

we say we're going to do something, we get it done. We reach out and include people in the community to get synergy. We "bootstrap" the process to make the most of every resource and force creative problem-solving. It is the same values we relied upon to develop Acceleron Learning. Anybody can throw money at a problem and make it work (maybe), but when you start with a big idea and a small budget, you have to learn how to be resourceful. It produces better results.

Through my upbringing and experiences like NASCAR, I knew I wanted to be an entrepreneur. I did my undergrad at Baylor, double majoring in entrepreneurship and financial planning. Next, I got my MBA at The Ohio State University, with duel concentrations in corporate strategy and marketing. While in business school, I had the opportunity to teach an intro to business course to undergrads that focused on soft skills. I found that many of the students were completely unaware and unprepared for navigating the realities of life. This exposed the need for something like Acceleron Learning, and it gave me some experience in teaching.

A grad-school internship with Burger King Corporation allowed me to work alongside the former Chief Marketing Officer, Russ Klein. He taught me about the power of being both a generalist and a specialist, and helped to get my professional career off the ground. After getting my MBA I worked as a corporate strategy consultant for Accenture, with a primary focus on marketing organization design for consumer goods and retail clients. Accenture taught me how to size up situations quickly, how to make smart business decisions, and how to deliver a quality work product. From a business perspective, I had the privilege of working with some of the smartest people on the planet: graduates from Ivy

League schools and the like. Despite this, I found that even these people lacked many practical life skills. The lesson? It doesn't matter where you are on the education or socio-economic spectrum, a practical life skills knowledge gap exists.

How did we produce hundreds of video lectures for Acceleron Learning? By making a feature film first! Before my parents moved from El Paso to Dallas (our headquarters), my dad had something he wanted to do—film the movie *Ilegales* (ilegalesthemovie.com). Having worked in Mexico for 25 years, he saw illegal immigration from a lot of different perspectives and wanted to highlight this important issue by telling the story through the eyes of the immigrants themselves. Making a film allowed us to "see how the sausage was made." I have a background in radio broadcasting and understand the fundamentals of good communication, but movie making is very different. We learned about filming, lighting, sound, scripting, acting, and all steps of the production process. So when we kicked around the idea of starting Acceleron Learning, we had the right skill set to create video lectures in-house.

My parents wanted to be closer to my sister (who was in college at Baylor) and me, so they moved to Dallas in late 2010. My dad and I had often talked about doing something together, and the timing was good for me to step away from Accenture. One afternoon, while driving down the road, we got into an intense conversation about how practical life skills are lacking in the lives of so many people, and how no one seemed to be addressing the problem. Then it just hit us: "We should do something about that!" **So we did.**

Our Thanks

acceleronlearning.com

I am blessed to have worked with a wonderful team of professionals in developing Acceleron Learning. All are exceptionally talented individuals who gave selflessly of their time and energy to make Acceleron Learning a reality and help refine it into a solid product. In no particular order, I would like mention a few of them: My wife Megan, Gregg Jackson, Becky Jackson, Kayla Jackson, Marc Ankerman, Jennifer Heckscher, Shawn Jackson, Scott Ballard, Eric Bowman, Murali Cheruvu, Kevin MacKenzie, Frank Nardelli, Dan Lopez, my close friends, and my entire community at The Village Church. I would like to call special attention to a few of the key contributors who helped forge Acceleron Learning:

Daniel Bodnar
Daniel is a close friend of mine who also happens to be a great programmer and web developer. As I say, he put the ".com" in Acceleron Learning. Daniel took hundreds of sheets of paper and made them into a living, breathing website. I cannot thank him enough for the late nights, early mornings, and for consistently going above and beyond to help make us successful. Daniel—Bus stop incident and all, I love ya, bro.

Nancy Batch
Nancy developed dozens of curriculum topics and conducted interviews for our Insights @Work podcasts. She teaches distance learning courses for Berkeley and others, but she's also a practitioner: a trained paralegal and CPA. My dad casually observed while standing in her home office, "Nancy, you have more degrees than a thermometer!" She is a constant source of inspiration and does nothing but quality work. Nancy—the next cup of coffee is on me.

Becky Fredrickson

When we started to look for young talent to deliver our K–12 video lectures, two kids (a brother and sister) came with their parents for tryouts. Their mother, Becky, took a keen interest in what we were doing. We were thrilled to learn that she is a professor at Texas Woman's University, specializing in education curriculum instruction and design. Becky has made many contributions, most significantly the development of all supplemental teaching materials and much of the research for this book. Her positive attitude and no-nonsense approach reminded me that all of the effort was worth it. Becky—there will always be a Diet Coke in my fridge with your name on it.

The Saulsberry Family

My parents' neighbors, Thelma and Thomas, helped with many activities along the way. Their kids did several of the lectures for our K–12 curriculum, Thelma helped to design quiz questions and unit descriptions, and Thomas did a great deal of work on the supplemental materials and on market research. Saulsberry Family—you are all first class.

Sam Ramsey, Jeremy Ottens, Connor Bynum, and Grant Wakefield

All of these guys are friends from church who also happen to be excellent video editors. Together, they are responsible for post-production on over 100 hours of video content for Acceleron Learning. They put in many late nights and dealt with a number of tough deadlines. Guys—thanks for bringing our products to life.

Lorena Pape

Lorena is our graphic designer extraordinaire. She's done over 4,000 PowerPoint slides, as well as branding for our products and the layout and design work on this book. She was an exceptional find and has acted as a true professional throughout. Lorena—I consider you one of our finest colleagues.

Tom and Margaret Hart

Margaret works at YouTube and her husband, Tom Hart and I met at Accenture. Tom and I share a passion for entrepreneurship, and he has done much to test my thinking and act as a sounding board during development. YouTube is positioned nicely to democratize education. We are excited to have a channel on their EDU platform and take part in that process. Tom and Margaret—thanks for your friendship and support!

Dr. Natalie Lundsteen, Director of Graduate Career Development at UT Southwestern Medical Center at Dallas

We got in touch with Natalie through one of my former colleagues at Accenture, Suzanne Pals. While working on the documentary for our website, we were looking for a workforce or human resources expert. We got connected with Natalie, who happened to work in career services at Stanford, and who got a Ph.D. at Oxford by studying internships and student readiness for the workforce. Her insight and work with the Gallup Organization on Wellbeing Finder have really sharpened the empirical credential of our product. Natalie—thanks for proving that super-smart people can also be super-practical people.

Sarah Michaels

We were looking for a script writer—someone who could turn dry content into something interesting—and we found Sarah. With experience writing scripts for online educational videos, Sarah was a perfect fit. More than 500,000 words later, she also made major contributions to our document repository and she made significant contributions to the writing of this book! Sarah—you have a way with words, and for that we are grateful.

Damen Lopez

My dad's new neighbor across the street just happens to run a company called No Excuses University. It works with public education to make college readiness a focal point in grades K–12. After telling him about Acceleron Learning, he said, why don't you start in kindergarten with this? Point taken. Damen was the inspiration for us to cascade our adult curriculum down to grades 7–9, 4–6, 1–3 and K. Damen also suggested we write this book to get the word out about Acceleron Learning. We are now working with NEU to provide Acceleron Learning content to over 6,500 teachers at nearly 200 public schools across America, reaching over 100,000 K–12 students. Damen—thanks for inspiring us and catching the vision in a big way.

Todd Imwalle

Todd was our initial window into the world of higher education, specifically at The University of Dayton and within the surrounding community. Both UD grads, my dad and Todd have spent many evenings reminiscing about their time in college and talking about how to make a positive impact on the next generation of students. Todd solidified our decision to include the Personal Wellness pillar, and has been a constant supporter every step of the way. Todd—your advocacy on our behalf is a great and thoughtful gift.

Accelerator Curriculum Listing

acceleronlearning.com

Accelerator Curriculum is over 200 video lectures designed to teach you practical life skills. The next several pages provide a complete listing (as of the printing of this book) of Accelerator Curriculum topics. Each item listed represents a video lecture, and is accompanied by robust supplemental materials for instruction and learning.

The premise: if experts had 30 minutes to teach you the essentials about a variety of practical life topics, what would they say? Written by subject-matter experts in each discipline, Accelerator Curriculum is divided into four main pillars. Each lecture is presented by a professional broadcaster, and includes a brief quiz to test your knowledge.

Adult Video Lecture Curriculum (Grades 10–12+)	
▸ Financial Literacy	▸ Legal Basics
▸ Career Dynamics	▸ Personal Wellness

Grade K–9 Video Lecture Curriculum	
▸ Grades 7–9	▸ Grades 1–3
▸ Grades 4–6	▸ Grade K

FINANCIAL LITERACY: ADULT UNITS

Financial Foundations
> ▸ **Types of Loans** – This unit discusses the various means of borrowing money as well as the general reasons for borrowing money.
> ▸ **Banking 101** – This unit describes the basics of consumer banking, such as the types of accounts offered and the types of financial institutions that offer banking services.
> ▸ **The Structure of a Loan** – This unit describes the structure and key components of a loan, including principal, interest rate, and payment terms.
> ▸ **Marketing & Consumerism** – This unit explores the relationship between reality and marketing hype, based on the U.S. consumerist culture.

- **Components of a Credit Score** – This unit discusses the various components of a credit score, the meaning of the range of scores available, and the impact your credit score has on your financial life.
- **The Credit Card Game** – This unit outlines ways to understand and manage credit card debt, and also discusses the cost of credit card debt.
- **Financial Ratios 101** – This unit discusses the significance of financial ratios, what they mean to your personal financial health, and how to calculate them.
- **Improving Your Ratios** – This unit describes the steps necessary to improve your personal financial ratios, which impacts your standing with lenders and your financial health.
- **Completing a 1040EZ** – This unit explores the components of a basic U.S. Individual tax return, called the Form 1040EZ.
- **Supply & Demand Theory** – This unit explores the relationship between supply and demand in a market-driven economy, and other basic economic principles.
- **Inflation & Interest** – This unit explores the relationship between economic inflation and interest rates.
- **GNP & Taxes** – This unit discusses the concept and components of Gross National Product, which is a measure of a nation's production. It also discusses sources and uses of tax revenues.
- **Philanthropy & Charity** – This unit describes the significance and financial impact of philanthropy, and the tax impact of charity.

Financial Instruments

- **Property/Casualty Insurance** – Property and casualty insurance both serve as a hedge against loss. This unit describes why you need it and how to get it.
- **Life & Health Insurance** – This unit covers the fundamentals of life and health insurance policies, including the different types of insurance available to consumers.
- **Stocks & Mutual Funds** – This unit explores the financial instruments known as stocks, or equities, which represent an ownership interest in a corporation.
- **Bonds, CDs, & Cash** – This unit explores the investment vehicles known as bonds, or "fixed income securities," and discusses cash and certificates of deposit from an investment perspective.
- **Retirement Account Types** – This unit covers a variety of financial instruments typically used for saving and growing retirement funds.

- **Retirement Strategies** – This unit explores different methods available for building assets that can be used to finance a comfortable retirement.
- **Transitioning to Retirement** – This unit will review tips and strategies to define your retirement, plan for the transition, align your finances, and develop any new skills that you might need.

Personal Budgeting

- **Build a Personal Budget** – A budget is a basic financial tool for planning. This unit explores the process of creating a personal budget using an Excel-based example.
- **Your Balance Sheet** – This unit explores the various components of a balance sheet, which is a summary of assets balanced against total liabilities and equity.
- **Fix Budget Shortfalls** – This unit discusses practical tips for managing your budget and reducing expenses if cash shortfalls occur.
- **Education Budgeting** – This unit explores how to budget, prepare for, and manage the costs of attending college.
- **Education Financial Aid** – This unit explores the costs of attending college, types of college funding, and the processes for applying for various forms of college aid.
- **Economics of a Graduate Degree** – This unit explores the process of pursuing and financing your graduate studies.
- **Buying & Selling a Car** – This unit looks at the factors involved in each step of the car-ownership process including buying, selling and maintaining a car.
- **Economics of Home Ownership** – This unit looks at the financial aspects of personal real estate transactions related to buying and selling a home.
- **Economics of a Spouse** – This unit discusses the economic implications of choosing a spouse and ways to think about the financial side of marriage.
- **Economics of Children** – This unit reviews the economic considerations of having and raising children.
- **The Affordable Wedding** – This unit discusses methods for planning a wedding while staying within a reasonable budget.
- **The Affordable Funeral** – This unit discusses the various tasks associated with funerals and specifically addresses ways to manage an affordable funeral.

CAREER DYNAMICS: ADULT UNITS

Building Your Brand

- **Your Mission & Brand** – This unit discusses the concept of branding as it applies to individuals, and how developing a personal mission statement can help you develop a personal brand.
- Your Value Proposition – This unit introduces the concept of a "value proposition," which is the core set of unique, quantifiable features that can help define a person or an organization.
- **Employment Trends** – This unit discusses the trends that impact the employment environment, how to analyze and respond to them.
- **The "Perfect" Résumé** – This unit discusses how to build the "perfect" résumé, from contents to formatting and delivery.
- **Path to a Career** – This unit discusses the types of education available to achieve your career goals and different types of post-secondary degrees.
- **College Readiness** – This unit describes what it takes to get into and succeed in higher education.
- **College Admissions** – This unit discusses how to get into college including choosing the right school, the application process, submitting great applications, and managing school choices.
- **College Campus Knowledge** – This unit explains how to navigate the typical college campus, from understanding the resources available to successfully engaging advisors, faculty, and support staff throughout your education experience.
- **Academic Course Work** – This unit discusses selecting a field of study, planning your schedule, and managing your academic course load in college.
- **Extracurricular Activities** – This unit offers a structured approach for selecting extracurricular activities in college, and explains how they relate to the skills that are valued by employers.
- **Work Experience & Skills** – This unit explores how to get a head start in building work experience and skills during college to include in your résumé.
- **How to Study** – This unit describes effective study habits and techniques.
- **Note & Test Taking** – This unit will teach you active listening techniques, note-taking strategies, and how to be an effective test-taker.
- **Research & Paper Writing** – This unit explains research

techniques and how to conceptualize, draft, and finalize a research paper.

- **Stand Out at Work** – This unit describes ways to make a positive impression at work and how to become well-read in the process.
- **Internship Success** – This unit addresses how to find internships and how students can make the most of the experience.
- **Move Up or Move On!** – This unit discusses the elements of focused intentional career development.

Job Search

- **Interviewing 101** – This unit discusses preparation techniques, typical formats, and tips for job interviewing. It is a summary of all other interviewing units.
- **Interview Preparation** – This unit discusses the process and techniques for preparing for an interview.
- **Interview Dos & Don'ts** – This unit covers the basic elements of a successful job interview.
- **Behavioral Interviewing** – This unit looks at the various techniques involved in navigating a behavioral interview by using the STAR technique.
- **Behavioral Interviewing Demo** – This unit provides a demonstration of a behavioral interview for a fictitious company, with suggestions and examples of thoughtful responses to interview questions.
- **Other Types of Interviews** – This unit discusses various other (not behavioral) types of interview techniques, such as phone screens, panel, and case interviews.
- **Career Fairs and Recruiting** – This unit discusses how to use career fairs and recruiting events to your advantage when searching for a position after graduation.
- **Networking and Cold Calling** – This unit explores the importance of networking, elevator pitches, and cold calling.
- **The Job Offer** – This unit discusses the decision-making process involved in evaluating and securing a job offer.
- **Job Lost and Found** – This unit explains how to effectively make a career or job transition, especially following a layoff or termination.

Managing People

- **Leadership** – This unit defines leadership traits and behaviors, and explains how to cultivate leadership in yourself and others.
- **Management Approaches** – This unit explores the various management styles found in the workplace, and how to use them effectively.

- **Incentive Structures** – This unit discusses how to motivate people using a variety of incentives.
- **Workplace Culture** – This unit discusses common workplace cultures, and offers advice on how to interact with them.
- **Business Etiquette** – This unit explains the set of written and unwritten rules of the workplace, known as business etiquette.
- **Running a Meeting** – This unit discusses methods of conducting different types of effective and efficient business meetings.
- **Work Style Synergy** – This unit explores how people work together to get things done, and the inherent work style differences you'll encounter in the workplace.
- **Negotiation & Bargaining** – This unit explores the concepts of bargaining and negotiation, the difference between the two, and the methods employed in both activities.
- **Conflict Management** – This unit discusses techniques for promoting positive conflict and managing negative conflict.
- **Customer Service** – This unit describes the value of customer service, how to put your customers first, and techniques for improved service levels.

Managing Work

- **Time Management** – This unit discusses how to exercise conscious control over the amount of time spent on specific activities.
- **Project Management** – This unit discusses the planning, organizing, directing, and controlling of resources in order to complete specific objectives.
- **Thinking Creatively** – This unit discusses the creative thinking process and addresses the different kinds of thinking, and the characteristics of creative people.
- **Defining the Problem** – This unit is the first of a three-part series on problem solving, and provides a methodology for focusing your definition of the problem that is to be solved.
- **Solving the Problem** – This unit is the second part of a three-part series on problem solving, and provides a number of tools for arriving at an answer/solution to the problem.
- **Communicating Ideas** – This unit is the third part of a three-part series on problem solving. Once the question has been answered, you must package and deliver results using effective communication.
- **Presentation Skills** – This unit discusses how to plan, prepare and deliver an effective presentation.
- **It's Not All Profit** – This unit discusses what happens to money

taken in by a corporation, and what a company must do to ensure profitability.

▸ **Think Like an Entrepreneur** – This unit describes the characteristics and unique perspective of an entrepreneur.

▸ **Starting a Small Business** – This unit describes the basics of developing and starting a small business.

LEGAL BASICS: ADULT UNITS

In Your Personal Life

▸ **The Legal System** – This unit analyzes the U.S. branches of government, discusses its adversarial system of justice, and reviews the civil and criminal process in the U.S. Court system.

▸ **Hiring an Attorney** – This unit covers the process of hiring an attorney and the attributes you should seek in one.

▸ **Elements of a Contract** – This unit is an introduction to the basic elements of a contract. The core topics are contract formation and interpretation, enforceability, performance, and breach of contract.

▸ **Common Contract Pitfalls** – This unit addresses some of the more common issues found in real estate contracts, consumer contracts and employment contracts, and discusses remedies for each.

▸ **Common Misdemeanors** – This unit is a survey of common misdemeanors and the respective processes and penalties in the United States.

▸ **Common Felonies** – This unit defines common felonies and the respective processes and penalties in the United States.

▸ **Civil Law** – This unit discusses the branch of law known as civil, or non-criminal, law. Specific attention is paid to the process, courts, and to civil causes of action.

▸ **Renting an Apartment** – This unit covers the many legal, social, and financial variables involved in successfully renting or leasing an apartment.

▸ **Buying & Selling a Home** – This unit reviews the process of leasing, buying and selling a home, and the pros and cons of owning real estate.

▸ **Estate Planning** – This unit teaches the elements of an estate and the basic documents that are imperative in estate planning.

▸ **Implications of Divorce** – This unit examines statutory law and principles relating to the formation and dissolution of marriage and families. Major topics include child custody, child support, visitation rights, spousal support, and the division of marital assets and liabilities.

▸ **Filing for Bankruptcy** – This unit discusses ways to avoid bankruptcy, the relief available to debtors under the Federal Bankruptcy statutes, the implications of filing.

▸ **A Vote of Confidence** – This unit describes the voting process, how to evaluate candidates for office, and how to make informed civic decisions.

In the Workplace

▸ **Intellectual Property** – This unit discusses legal instruments for intellectual property, such as trademarks, patents and copyrights. It will help you to identify, protect, and avoid infringement of these in the workplace.

▸ **Employment Law** – Federal and state employment laws offer employees certain protections and securities from the unfair treatment and discriminatory actions of the employer. This unit identifies and addresses common complaints raised by the employee and the available remedies for them.

▸ **Ethics in the Workplace** – This unit helps you determine what ethical considerations are important on a job and how you should address ethical issues involving co-workers.

▸ **White Collar Crime** – This unit provides an overview of the types, impacts and penalties associated with corporate/workplace criminal activity.

PERSONAL WELLNESS: ADULT UNITS

Mental Health

▸ **Depression** – This unit looks at the diagnosis and treatment of the mood disorder known as depression.

▸ **Emotional Health** – This unit covers the characteristics of emotional health, as well as treatment for emotional health issues, and strategies for achieving emotional wellness.

▸ **Work Ethic & Tenacity** – This unit teaches you how to cultivate a good work ethic, and how to persevere in the face of adversity.

▸ **Stress & Anxiety** – This unit discusses stress and anxiety: The mental, physical, and emotional reactions to a situation, event, or activity.

▸ **Addictions & Drug Use** – This unit covers the causes, symptoms and treatments of addiction and drug use, including common addictions and the underlying characteristics.

▸ **Eating Disorders** – This unit covers diagnosis and treatment of abnormal eating habits.

▸ **Mental Illness** – This unit discusses mental illness, including the origins, impacts, and specific characteristics of different conditions.

▸ **Suicide Awareness** – This unit looks at the warning signs of suicide, what to do if someone is considering suicide, and actions you can take to help prevent it.

▸ **Religion and Spirituality** – This unit offers a method for examining religious belief systems, and examines the social and personal wellness benefits of spirituality.

Physical Health

▸ **Balanced Nutrition** – This unit looks at balanced nutrition, including the basics of nutrition and how to achieve proper nutrition and diet.

▸ **A Workout that Works** – This unit covers the components of an exercise program that will get you in shape and keep you in shape.

▸ **Checkup or Check Out** – This unit discusses the importance of medical examinations as a way to stay healthy and diagnose issues.

▸ **Sleep Does a Body Good** – This unit looks at the science of sleep and why you likely need more.

▸ **A Healthy Environment** – This unit discusses the factors that create or effect a healthy physical environment, and ways to reduce exposure to common pollutants.

Social Health

▸ **Workplace Dynamics** – This unit discusses the various components, or dynamics and interactions, of the work environment.

▸ **Your Social Network** – This unit discusses the importance of social networks, both online and offline, and how to build and maintain them.

▸ **Bullying** – This unit looks at the problem of bullying in school and the workplace, and offers options for addressing the issue and resolving conflict.

▸ **Appreciating the Arts** – This unit discusses ways to appreciate the arts by defining and assessing artistic expression.

- **Volunteering** – This unit addresses several aspects of volunteering including the types of volunteers, the benefits of volunteering, and how to prevent burnout as a volunteer.
- **Dating Dynamics** – This unit discusses how to evaluate and manage stages of the dating process.
- **A Marriage Built to Last** – This unit discusses the characteristics of a strong marriage that will last through thick and thin, and how to foster such a relationship.
- **Family Dynamics** – This unit discusses family dynamics and how to build and sustain a healthy family environment.
- **Impacts of Divorce** – This unit discusses the prevalence of divorce in the United States, and looks at the health risks of divorce for adults and children.
- **Aging & The Elderly** – This unit addresses the aging process, medical and social conditions facing the elderly, how to help and elderly relative, and issues related to the elderly population.
- **Death & Grieving** – This unit describes the process of dying, final arrangements, grieving and resilience, and estate planning.

UNITS FOR K–12

The Accelerator Curriculum K–12 product includes over 110 video lectures for Grades 10–12 from our adult curriculum, and another 90 video lectures, specially designed for Grades K–9. This curriculum is fully integrated to provide *"cascade"* learning as a student moves through school. For example, Grade 7–9 lecture units are distilled from Grade 10–12 (Adult Units), and so on, for truly integrated learning by age group.

Grades 7–9
These specially-designed middle school units are delivered by high school-aged lecturers, and are 30 minutes in length.

- **Financial Literacy (6 Units)**
  - Economics
  - Basic Financial Concepts
  - Protecting Your Money
  - Growing Your Money
  - Money Management
  - Major Life Decisions
- **Legal Basics (6 Units)**
  - The Legal System
  - Hiring an Attorney
  - Ethics
  - Workplace Rules
  - Legal Transactions
  - Dealing with Legal Issues

▶ **Career Dynamics (11 Units)**
- The Career Environment
- Defining Who You Are
- Guiding and Motivating
- Relate and Communicate
- Planning Your Work
- Creative Problem Solving
- Gathering Experience
- Job Search
- Career Path Compass
- Preparing for College
- Making the Grade

▶ **Personal Wellness (7 Units)**
- Healthy Mental Habits
- Dealing with Mental Issues
- Healthy Physical Habits
- Dealing with Physical Issues
- Healthy Social Habits
- Dealing with Social Issues
- Bullying

Grades 4–6

These specially-designed upper-elementary school units are delivered by middle school-aged lecturers, and are 20 minutes in length.

▶ **Financial Literacy (5 Units)**
- Our Economy
- Basic Money Concepts
- Banking
- Budgeting Your Money
- Shopping Basics

▶ **Legal Basics (5 Units)**
- What is the Legal System?
- Working with the Legal System
- What are Ethics?
- Rules and Procedures
- Legal Issues

▶ **Career Dynamics (9 Units)**
- The World Around You
- Who You Are
- Working with Others
- What is Communication?
- Prep for School Success
- Solving Problems
- Look Towards the Future
- Careers and College
- Making the Grade

▶ **Personal Wellness (9 Units)**
- Keep Your Mind Healthy
- Talk About Problems
- Keep Your Body Healthy
- Eating and Exercising
- Staying Healthy
- Making Friends
- Families and Social Issues
- Helping Others
- Bullying

Grades 1–3
These specially-designed lower-elementary school units are delivered by middle school-aged lecturers, and are 15 minutes in length.

▸ **Financial Literacy (2 Units)**
  - Our Economy
  - Basic Money Concepts

▸ **Legal Basics (4 Units)**
  - What is the Legal System?
  - The Legal System at Work
  - What are Ethics?
  - Rules and Procedures

▸ **Career Dynamics (7 Units)**
  - The World Around You
  - Who You Are
  - Working with Others
  - What is a Good Student?
  - Solving Problems
  - Planning Your Future
  - Making the Grade

▸ **Personal Wellness (8 Units)**
  - Keep Your Mind Healthy
  - Talk About Problems
  - Keep Your Body Healthy
  - Eating and Exercising
  - Making Friends
  - Families
  - Helping Others
  - Bullying

Grade K
These specially-designed kindergarten units are delivered by middle school-aged lecturers, and are 15 minutes in length.

▸ **Financial Literacy (2 Units)**
  - Dollars and Cents
  - Basic Money Concepts

▸ **Legal Basics (3 Units)**
  - What is the Legal System?
  - What are Ethics?
  - Rules and Procedures

▸ **Career Dynamics (6 Units)**
  - The World Around You
  - Who You Are
  - Working with Others
  - Solving Problems
  - Exploring Jobs
  - Making the Grade

▸ **Personal Wellness (6 Units)**
  - Keeping Your Mind Healthy
  - Keeping Your Body Healthy
  - Making Friends
  - Families
  - Helping Others
  - Bullying

Endnotes

acceleronlearning.com

Introduction: It's Not Rocket Surgery

1. *One of the things ...agree*: reference (McKinsey, 2013, pp. 39, 40, & 67).

2. *Amid a...on a project*: reference (Korn, 2013).

3. *The folks at Gallup ...for each essential element*: reference (Harter & Rath, 2010, pp. 117–118).

4. *Gallup's hundreds of business clients...leadership*: reference (Clifton, J. and Daniels, M., 2013).

5. *We've discussed...and they like it*: reference (Hodges, 2012).

Chapter 1: Hugh Dunno

1. *You can't graduate from ...financial management and nutrition*: reference (as cited in Acceleron Learning Documentary, 2011).

Chapter 3: The Hole Problem

1. *80% of a person's success ...20% comes from technical skills*: reference (Davis, 2009).

2. *It's because college kids...of office life"*: reference (White, M.C. 2013).

3. *If provosts could grade themselves...in the workplace*: reference (Grasgreen, 2014).

4. *Students and employers...degree*: reference (Grasgreen, 2013).

5. *Janette Marx...a competitive workforce*: reference (Banerjee, 2014).

6. *All sustained episodes...long-term growth*: reference (Rodrik, 2013).

7. *A 2011 poll showed...half of what it was a decade ago.* Only 15 percent of Americans say they trust the government in Washington to do what's right always or most of the time...Before the recession hit that number was usually in the low-to-mid 30's, and slightly more than a decade ago, it was in the high 30's or occasionally just over 40 percent: reference (CNN Poll, 2011).

8. *In the contemporary culture...expectations*: reference (Sayers, 2012).

Chapter 4: Financial Illiteracy

1. *A 2012 poll found ...with the same results.* A Bloomberg National Poll conducted March 8 through March 11, 2012 by Selzer & Company surveyed 1,002 adults across the United States on what they thought the most critical problem this nation is dealing with at present. The majority, 42%, responded with "unemployment and jobs" while "the federal deficit" came in second at 21% (PollingReport.com, 2012). In March 2011 this same question was asked of 1,001 adults across the U.S. and the results were similar— "unemployment and jobs" came in first at 43% and "federal deficit and spending" came in second at 29%: reference (PollingReport.com, 2012).

2. *As of the writing...approaching $18 trillion and climbing*: reference (U.S. National Debt Clock, 2014).

3. *An article in the Washington Times ... fiscal year through 2021. President Obama projects U.S. deficit spending will continue to ring in at $1 trillion each fiscal year through 2021*: reference (Dinan, 2012).

4. *If you were to try ... would take 32,000 years*: reference (Coleman, 2011).

5. *To balance the budget ...have riots like Greece*: Spending for mandatory programs [i.e. Social Security, Medicare, and federal pensions] and interest is greater than the tax revenues collected... After the checks are processed for mandatory programs and interest there isn't one dollar left to fund the military or any federal employee or departmental office: reference (Mason, 2012).

6. *An article in Forbes Magazine ...basic compound interest problem*: Only 50% of respondents were able to answer the first two questions correctly and less than a third was able to answer all three. In a related study less than 18% of people surveyed were able to answer a simple two-period compound interest problem: reference (Cooley, 2010).

7. *A financial literacy survey ...how to keep a budget*: A 2012 NFCC financial literacy survey found "60% [of] 18 to 34 year-olds [are] not keeping a budget": reference (Malcom, 2012).

8. *The United States' Secretary ...financial literacy issue*: reference (Malcom, 2012).

9. *Whether they're learning...lean more on social programs*: reference (Malcom, 2012).

10. *A majority of young...few signs of improving*: reference (Malcom, 2012).

11. *This is especially...student loans to mortgages*: reported in a PNC survey (Malcom, 2012).

12. *Unemployment for those...rate of 8.2%*: according to BLS data from March 2012 (Malcom, 2012).

13. *Data analysis ...45% in 1993*: reference (Martin & Lehren, 2012).

14. *The Project...$29,400 in student loan debt*: reference (Student Debt and, 2012).

15. *The credit card...Diners Club Card*: reference (Woolsey & Gerson, 2009).

16. *Credit cards act as ...which is off in the distant future*: reference (Harter & Rath, 2010, p. 203).

17. *When people feel sad ...bad financial choices.* Gallup conducted a broad study, including people from more than 150 countries on what factors are most important in determining a person's wellbeing over the course of their life. The results of the study are included in the Wellbeing book by Gallup: When we are feeling down, trying to cheer ourselves up by going on a personal shopping spree is unlikely to help in the long run. Sadness may even lead us to spend a lot more

money on ourselves than we otherwise would...Even though we don't realize it, a bad mood could lead to a cascade of poor financial decisions...[Their] research suggests that the worst time to make a major purchase is when you are feeling down. We spend the most when we feel the worst. So much for "retail therapy": reference (Harter & Rath, 2010, p. 54-55).

18. *According to a financial literacy poll ...denial for Americans*: reference (Bankrate.com, 2004).

19. *The Federal Reserve Bank ...home equity lines of credit*: reference (Bauer & Nash, 2012).

20. *Data released Tuesday...already happened*: reference: (Frizell, 2014).

21. *In states...standards*: reference (Bernard, 2010).

22. *But they're not doing it ...mastery of financial literacy*: reference (Malcom, 2012).

Chapter 5: Career Ineffectiveness

1. *Gallup's work showed... a person's overall wellbeing*: reference (Harter & Rath, 2010, pp. 16, 20, 21, 23–25).

2. *Researchers for Gallup's Wellbeing Finder... with a firm yes*: reference (Harter & Rath, 2010, p. 15).

3. *Eighty percent of college-bound students ... during their college years*: reference (as cited in Acceleron Learning Documentary, 2011).

4. *A study found that less... accumulate thousands of dollars of debt*: reference (Carey, Hess, Kelly, & Schneider, 2012).

6. *Not only that, you're...84 percent of student loans*: reference (as cited in Acceleron Learning Documentary, 2011).

7. *Taxpayers have paid billions of dollars... lost federal and state income taxes*: reference (as cited in Acceleron Learning Documentary, 2011).

8. *From 1985 to 2011... during that same timeframe*: reference (Wadsworth, 2011).

9. *Most of the growth...instructional staff*: reference (Reynolds, 2014).

10. *Debt from student loans... don't believe they can pay it back*: reference (Yerak, 2012).

11. *People age 40 and older... nation's total student loan debt*: reference (Watson, 2012).

12. *According to U.S. News & World Report... column to the left*: reference (Graves, 2014).

13. *However, the most popular bachelor's degree... column to the right*: reference ("Top 10 College Majors" 2014).

14. *Young adults with bachelor's degrees... mounting student loans*: reference (Yen, 2012).

15. *Just 44% of college graduates... working below their educational level*: reference (Watson, 2011).
16. *Nearly 30%...degree*: reference (Marcus, 2013).
17. *Americans under 25...the recession*: reference (Casselman, B. and Walker, M. 2013).
18. *The job market... low demand for liberal arts degrees*: reference (Yen, 2012).
19. *Ann...Sincerely, Barack Obama*: reference (Brooks, 2014).
20. *In 2012 the median salary... is a bachelor's degree*: reference ("Occupational Outlook Handbook," 2012).
21. *In 2012 the median pay for actors... aren't that lucky*: reference ("Occupational Outlook Handbook," 2012).
22. *There is no proof...salary*: reference (Korn, 2014).
23. *The entire multibillion-dollar...college!*: reference (Flanagan, 2014).
24. *In an article titled... range anywhere from 1% to 190%*: reference (Marquit, 2012).
25. *Several factors... which college you attended*: reference (Marquit, 2012).
26. *After two years of training... total net earnings is $53,025*: reference (Salary.com, 2012).
27. *Can provide job security, credibility, and increased earnings potential*: reference (Guina, 2009).
28. *For example, a civil engineer... for gifted and talented children*: reference (Careeronestop Certification Finder Tool, 2012).
29. *Students aren't prepared... how to find a mentor*: reference (as cited in Acceleron Learning Documentary, 2011).
30. *Employers are looking for candidates... relevant experience in their desired field*: According to Kathy Hatem, VP Resourcing at HSBC Bank, "The best candidate isn't always the person with the highest GPA, you look at balance, involvement in all areas: education, work experience, internships, extracurricular activities": reference (Acceleron Learning Documentary, 2011).
31. *College internships allow... for getting a job today*: reference ("College Internships," 2012).
32. *A study showed that "students who had... those not doing one ($28,000)"*: reference (Godofsky, Van Horn, & Zukin, 2011).
33. *The value of internships... getting a job after graduation*: reference (Watson, 2011).
34. *According to the Bureau of Labor Statistics... job openings*: reference (as cited in Petrecca, 2010).
35. *Only 49% of graduates... three years prior*: reference (Korn & Weber, 2012).

36. *Fewer than half of employers... and 79% in 2007*: reference (Petrecca, "Toughest Test," 2010).

37. *Another report showed... were employed full time*: reference (Godofsky, Van Horn, & Zukin, 2011).

38. *Recently a friend...just by showing up*: reference (Brunner, 2011).

39. *Further, the author of...thirty-odd years*: reference (Ablow, 2013).

40. *The cost to employers of training each new hire is $40,000*: reference (Gil, 2011).

Chapter 6: Legal Illiteracy

1. *In recent years...$809 per person*: reference (Association of Trial Lawyers of America, 2012).

2. *Today's entitlement culture... for private aggrandizement*: reference (Will, 2009).

3. *67 percent... when something goes wrong*: the study was performed by Harris Interactive: reference (Corso & Shores, 2005).

4. *According to maritalstatus.com... amounts to $28-billion each year*: reference (McDonald, 2001).

5. *I see many... for this company anymore*: reference (as cited in Acceleron Learning Documentary, 2011).

6. *The number of civil lawsuits filed in fiscal year (FY) 2010... increase from FY 2009*: reference (Filings in the Federal, 2011).

7. *In 2010, the U.S. bankruptcy courts received... took effect*: reference (Filings in the Federal, 2011).

8. *Another growing area for lawsuits in the United States is medical malpractice*: reference (Statistics on Medical Malpractice, 2008).

9. *Physicians order more... medical malpractice lawsuits*: reference (Park, 2012).

10. *Many of these tests are unwarranted, and sometimes even harmful to patients*: reference (Park, 2012).

11. *The Federal Bureau of Investigation... annual cost of $300 to $660 billion*: reference (NW3C, 2012).

12. *According to Lawyers.com... fresh out of law school*: reference (Lawyers.com, 2012).

13. *Compared to rural areas... and legal secretaries*: reference (Lawyers.com, 2012).

14. *Total costs for a civil lawsuit can range from $25,000 to $50,000*: The Business Lawyers law firm estimated that the total cost for a civil lawsuit can range from $25,000 for legal defense before going to trial, and up to an additional $25,000 to go to trial: reference (Taylor, 2010)

Chapter 7: Personal Illness

1. *A new statistic from the Centers for Disease Control... average of 78.7 years*: reference (Gardner, 2012).

2. *Average life expectancies for Americans were... and 76.8 in 2000*: reference (Frieden, Sebelius, & Sondik, 2011, p. 152).

3. *With the increased incidence... people getting sicker younger*: reference (Gardner, 2012).

4. *Many of our health care problems... healthy lifestyle choices*: reference (Mackey, 2009).

5. *The average American diet...7% of fruits and vegetables*: reference (Mackey, 2009).

6. *A survey... candy increased by 180%*: reference (Lobb, 2005).

7. *To supersize has become an accepted verb*: reference (Fenster, 2012).

8. *The foods Americans supersize...to our detriment*: reference (Fenster, 2012).

9. *In the Gallup Wellbeing study... five days a week*: reference (Harter & Rath, 2010, p. 78).

10. *While some nations... worst at 33%*: reference (Harter & Rath, 2010, p. 87).

11. *Childhood obesity is accelerating... the past 20 years*: reference (Sofsian, 2007).

12. *Statistics show that 63% of the American population is overweight*: reference (Sofsian, 2007).

13. *According to USA Today...cost the United States $270 billion each year*: reference (as cited in Acceleron Learning Documentary, 2011).

14. *The Gallup Organization reported that... control Diabetes symptoms by 43%*: reference (Harter & Rath, 2010, p. 88).

15. *Getting a good night's sleep is like hitting a reset button*: reference (Harter & Rath, 2010, p. 81).

16. *Currently, people are getting... difficulty concentrating on tasks*: reference (Harter & Rath, 2010, p. 81–82).

17. *For example, health insurance...expected to reach $25,000*: reference (Harter & Rath, 2010, p. 86).

18. *A 2007 Harvard study showed that "62%...a medical cause"*: reference (Harter & Rath, 2010, p. 87).

19. *A study by the Centers for Disease Control revealed "enough narcotics...every day for a month"*: reference ("Prescription Drug Deaths," 2012).

20. *This ultimately exacerbates...mental health problems*: reference (National Consortium on Stigma and Empowerment, 2010).

21. *More than 90 percent...diagnosable mental disorder*: reference (National Institute on Mental Health, 2014).

22. *We seem lonely... it's time to talk*: reference (Turkle, 2012).

23. *Looks to...engenders*: reference (Seaman, 2010).

24. *Contemporary culture...naïve hell*: reference (Sayers, 2010, p. 106).

25. *Points out...unrelated things*: reference (Churnin, 2013).

Chapter 9: Mia Culpa

1. *In fact...expressed that in 2006*: reference (Crim, 2009).

2. *In the...was cut down to 18 hours*: reference (Crim, 2009).

3. *We often...wellbeing*: reference (Harter & Rath, 2010, p. 153).

4. *Did you know...throughout college*: reference (as cited in Acceleron Learning Documentary, 2011).

5. *Sixty-six percent of students... influenced by friends and family*: reference (College Parents of America, 2011).

6. *The U.S. Census Bureau... fiscal year 2009*: reference (Fox News, "Public school per," 2011).

7. *And really, it's...No Child Left Behind Act*: reference (Fox News, "Public school per," 2011).

8. *More than you might...going it alone*: reference (Hartner & Rath, 2010, p. 93-104).

9. *The Association of American Colleges and Universities...skills for success*: reference (Parker, 2011).

10. *A recent CNN report... movie theaters and tanning salons*: reference (Parker, 2011).

11. *This has a formal name...President Reagan's secretary of education*: reference (Kix, 2012).

12. *Recently, a joint study... provided a fair assessment*: reference (Kix, 2012).

13. Their findings showed "The schools...that didn't": reference (Kix, 2012).

14. *A surge in spending... percent for instruction*: reference (Crabb, 2010).

15. *Faced with declining state funding...concentrated in athletics*: reference (Bachman, 2013)

16. *The indicators we use to capture..."graduation rate performance"*: reference (Morse & Flanigan, 2011).

17. *Big-name schools like... on nonacademic services*: reference (Crabb, 2010).

18. *The Labor Department...1970*: reference (Marklein, 2013).

19. *YouTube has also...views*: reference (Finn, 2012).

20. *Another is Khan Academy... unique hits each month*: reference (Finn, 2012).

21. *Even within...institutions*: reference (Koppel & Belkin, 2012).

22. *In a Personal Finance Employee Education Foundation study...at work!*: reference (Connor, 2012).

23. *If you lead or manage people... ability to grow*: reference (Harter & Rath, 2010, p. 133).

24. *Top performers... best for the organization*: reference (Harter & Rath, 2010, p. 135).

Chapter 10: Gaining Traction

1. *About 43 percent...in the past*: reference (Rampell, 2011).

2. *A study at the University of Indiana...conversation*: reference (Gordon, 2014).

3. *Ohio in the bottom quartile*: reference (Gallup, 2014).

APPENDIX C

References

acceleronlearning.com

▸ Ablow, K. (2013, January 8). We are raising a generation of deluded narcissists. Retrieved from: http://www.foxnews.com/opinion/2013/01/08/are-raising-generation-deluded-narcissists/

▸ Acceleron Learning Documentary (2011, November 1). *Life Experience in America*. Retrieved from: http://www.acceleronlearning.com

▸ AFP. (2012). Education channel on YouTube. Retrieved from: http://thestar.com.my/education/story.asp?file=/2012/3/18/education/10909037&sec=education

▸ Association of Trial Lawyers of America (2012, May 1). Civil lawsuit statistics. Retrieved from: http://www.statisticbrain.com/civil-lawsuit-statistics/

▸ Bachman, R. (2013). Colorado state university bets on a stadium to fill coffers. Retrieved from: http://online.wsj.com/news/articles/SB10001424052702303983904579093432304563144?mod=rss_mobile_uber_feed&mg=reno64-wsj

▸ Banerjee, R. (2014). Two sides of the same coin: The employment crisis and the education crisis. Retrieved from: http://www.forbes.com/sites/ashoka/2014/03/04/two-sides-of-the-same-coin-the-employment-crisis-and-the-education-crisis/

▸ Bauer, A. R., & Nash, B. J. (2012). Where are households in the deleveraging cycle? *The Federal Reserve Bank of Richmond*. Retrieved from: http://www.richmondfed.org/publications/research/economic_brief/2012/pdf/eb_12-01.pdf

▸ Bauer, R. A., & Nash, B. J., (2012). Where are households in the deleveraging cycle? Retrieved from: http://www.richmondfed.org/publications/research/economic_brief/2012/pdf/eb_12-01.pdf

▸ Bernard, T. S. (2010, April 9). Working financial literacy in with the three R's. Retrieved from: http://www.nytimes.com/2010/04/10/your-money/10money.html?_r=0

▸ Brooks, K. (2014). President Obama sends handwritten apology to art history professor. Retrieved from: http://www.huffingtonpost.com/2014/02/18/obama-art-history_n_4809007.html?icid=maing-grid7%7chtmlws-sb-bb%7cdl3%7csec1_lnk3%26pLid%3D444100

▸ Brunner, M. (2011). Growing up when 'everyone wins,' how do kids learn to win? Retrieved from: http://www.forbes.com/sites/forbesleadershipforum/2011/11/09/growing-up-when-everyone-wins-how-do-kids-learn-to-win

▸ Bureau of Labor Statistics, U.S. Department of Labor, Occupational Outlook Handbook, 2012-13 Edition, "Petroleum Engineers" and "Actors" search results (2012). Retrieved from: http://www.bls.gov/ooh/architecture-and-engineering/petroleum-engineers.htm and http://www.bls.gov/ooh/entertainment-and-sports/actors.htm

▸ Careeronestop Certification Finder Tool: http://www.acinet.org/certifications_new/cert_search_occupation.aspx

▸ Carey, K., Hess, F. M., Kelly, A., & Schneider, M. (2012). Study shows less that 55% of college students graduate in 6 years. Retrieved from: http://uncc49er.com/588/study-shows-less-than-55-of-college-students-graduate-in-6-years

▸ Casselman, B. and Walker, M. (2013). Wanted: Jobs for the New 'Lost' Generation. Retrieved from: http://online.wsj.com/news/articles/SB10001424127887323893004579057063223739696?mod=WSJ_WSJ_US_News_5&mg=reno64-wsj

▸ Churnin, Nancy. Build up your brain with help of expert: Center for Brain Health director says slow down, dig deeper. The Dallas Morning News, Section E. Front Page.

▸ Clark, K. (2011). College costs climb, yet again. Retrieved from: http://money.cnn.com/2011/10/26/pf/college/college_tuition_cost/index.htm

▸ Clifton, J. and Daniels, M. (2013). A real measure of higher ed. success. Retrieved from: http://online.wsj.com/news/articles/SB10001424052702304403804579261893126434068

▸ CNN Poll: Trust in government at all time low. (2011). Retrieved from: http://politicalticker.blogs.cnn.com/2011/09/28/cnn-poll-trust-in-government-at-all-time-low

▸ Coleman, D. (2011). GJ man: US debt situation worse than anyone thinks: Man crunches budget, finds "shocking numbers." Retrieved from: http://www.kjct8.com/news/29446257/detail.html

▸ College Parents of America. (2011). When your college student changes major. Retrieved from: http://www.collegeparents.org/members/resources/articles/when-your-college-student-changes-majors

▸ Connor, C. (2012). Employees Really Do Waste Time at Work, Part II. Retrieved from: http://www.forbes.com/sites/cherylsnappconner/2012/11/15/employees-really-do-waste-time-at-work-part-ii/

▸ Cooley, T. F. (2010, January 13). America's financial illiteracy. Retrieved from: http://www.forbes.com/2010/01/12/cfpa-financial-illiteracy-credit-cards-opinions-columnists-thomas-f-cooley.html

▸ Corso, R. and Shores, E. (2005, June 20). Public trust of civil justice. Retrieved from: http://www.instituteforlegalreform.com/get_ilr_doc.php?fn=Public%20trust%20of%20civil%20justice.pdf

▸ Crabb, N. (2010, August 24). $16.3M rec center opens today. *The Gainesville Sun*. Retrieved from: http://www.gainesville.com/article/20100824/ARTICLES/8241011?p=2&tc=pg

▸ Crim, D. (2009). Report says Americans spending less time with their families. Retrieved from: http://addins.whig.com/blogs/uponfurtherreview/2009/06/report-says-americans-spending-less-time-with-their-families

▸ Davis, E. (2009). Trendwatcher: Soft skills by any other name. Retrieved from: http://www.hrworld.com/features/trendwatcher-soft-skills-112309/

▸ De Vizard, P. (2010). The concern on stress and the rise of cardiovascular diseases. Retrieved from: http://ezinearticles.com/?The-Concern-on-Stress-and-the-Rise-of-Cardiovascular-Diseases&id=5172109

▸ Dinam, S. (2012, March 8). Govt. sets record deficit in February. *Washington Times*. Retrieved from: http://www.washingtontimes.com/news/2012/mar/8/govt-sets-record-deficit-february

▸ Fenster, M.S. (2012). We're living longer than ever before, but are we healthier? Retrieved from: http://www.theatlantic.com/health/archive/2011/09/were-living-longer-than-ever-before-but-are-we-healthier/245409

▸ Figart, D. M. & Niemiec, S. (2012, April 26). Debt from student loans is crippling a generation. Retrieved from: http://blog.nj.com/njv_guest_blog/2012/04/debt_from_student_loans_is_cri.html

▸ Filings in the federal judiciary continued to grow in fiscal year 2010. (2011). Retrieved from: http://www.uscourts.gov/News/NewsView/11-03-15/Filings_in_the_Federal_Judiciary_Continued_to_Grow_in_Fiscal_Year_2010.aspx

▸ Finn, H. (2012). Watching the ivory tower topple: New online course open to all constitute a thrilling collegiate coup. Retrieved from: http://online.wsj.com/article/SB10001424052702304636404577293430981335366.html

▸ Fisher, D. (2011). Models – course development: Instructional design --the taxonomy table. Retrieved from: http://oregonstate.edu/ instruct/coursedev/models/id/taxonomy/#table

▸ Flanagan, C. (2014). The Dark Power of Fraternities. Retrieved from: http://www.theatlantic.com/features/archive/2014/02/ the-dark-power-of-fraternities/357580/.

▸ Foley, R. L. (n.d.) Knowledge is power for bankruptcy, Steve Jobs and our world in general. Retrieved from: http://www. bankruptcylawnetwork.com/knowledge-is-power-for-bankruptcy-steve-jobs-and-our-world-in-general

▸ Fox News. (2011). Public school per-student spending increases as state funding decreases. Retrieved from: http://www.foxnews.com/ politics/ 2011/05/26/public-school-student-spending-increases-state-funding-decreases

▸ Frieden, T. R., Sebelius, K., Sondik, E. J. (2011). Health, United States, 2010: with special feature on death and dying (p 152). Retrieved from: http://www.cdc.gov/nchs/data/hus/hus10.pdf

▸ Frizell, S. (2014, February 19). Americans are taking on debt at scary rates. Retrieved from: http://time.com/8740/federal-reserve-debt-bankrate-consumers-credit-card/

▸ Gallup-Healthways (2014). State of American Wellbeing: 2013 State Rankings and Analysis. Retrieved from: http://info.healthways.com/ wbi2013

▸ Gardner, A. (2012, January 12). Americans living longer, report finds. *USA Today*. Retrieved from: http://www.usatoday.com/news/ health/story/health/story/2012-01-12/Americans-living-longer-report-finds/52513006/1

▸ Gibbons, V. (2012, April). How to pay off college debt. *Real Simple*, 144.

▸ Gil, A. (2011). Managing the cost of employee training. Retrieved from: http://www.articlesnatch.com/Article/Managing-The-Cost-Of-Employee-Training/637016

▸ Godofsky, J., Zukin, C., Van Horn, C. (2011). Unfulfilled expectations: Recent college graduates struggle in a troubled economy. Rutgers University. Retrieved from: http://www.heldrich. rutgers.edu/sites/default/files/content/Work_Trends_May_2011.pdf

▸ Gordon, A. (2014). Killing Pigs and Weed Maps: The Mostly Undread World of Academic Papers. Retrieved from: http://www.psmag.

com/navigation/books-and-culture/killing-pigs-weed-maps-mostly-unread-world-academic-papers-76733/

▶ Grasgreen, A. (2014). Ready or not. Retrieved from: http://www.insidehighered.com/news/2014/02/26/provosts-business-leaders-disagree-graduates-career-readiness#.Uw4DCWnkz04.email□

▶ Grasgreen, A. (2013). Qualified in their own minds. Retreived from: http://www.insidehighered.com/news/2013/10/29/ more-data-show-students-unprepared-work-what-do-about-it#ixzz2wL9NN24V

▶ Guina, R. (2009). Professional licenses and certifications can increase your marketability and salary. Retrieved from: http://cashmoneylife.com/professional-licenses-and-certifications-can-increase-your-marketability-and-salary

▶ Harter, J., & Rath, T. (2010) *Wellbeing: The Five Essential Elements*. New York, New York: Gallup Press.

▶ Hill, J. (n.d.). On-campus stadium getting a closer look. Retrieved from: http://www.baylor.edu/nation/index.php?id=86134

▶ Hodges, T. (2012). Email exchange between Gallup Consulting Research Director and Acceleron Learning. Retrieved from: http://www.outlook.com

▶ Houston, D. C. (2012). Baylor reports large increase in applications. *The Baylor Lariat*, 113(43), 1,7. Retrieved from: http://www.baylor.edu/content/services/document.php/173037.pdf

▶ Kamenetz, A. (2012). Obama should push bankruptcy relief for student loans. Retrieved from: http://www.cnn.com/2012/04/26/opinion/kamenetz-obama-higher-education/index.html

▶ Kix, P. (2012, April 22). Over a barrel on college costs. *The Dallas Morning News*, 1P, 5P.

▶ Koppel, N. & Belkin, D. (2012, October 7). Texas Pushes $10,000 Degree. *The Wall Street Journal*, Education. Retrieved from: http://online.wsj.com/article/SB10000872396390443493304578039040237714224.html

▶ Korn, M. & Weber, L. (2012, May). For Most Graduates, grueling job hunt awaits. The Wall Street Journal Online. Retrieved from: http://online.wsj.com/article/SB1000142405270230402010457738441032339198.html

▶ Korn, Melissa. (2013, March 7). The business of boot camps. The Wall Street Journal. Retrieved from: http://online.wsj.com/article/SB

1000142412788732417890457834041413385 8572.html?KEYWORDS
=business+of+boot+camps

▸ Korn, Melissa. (2014, March 17). Colleges are tested by push to
prove graduates' career success. Retrieved from: http://online.wsj.
com/news/articles/SB100014240527023035462045794350506842946
42?mod=WSJ_hpp_MIDDLENexttoWhatsNewsThird&mg=reno64-
wsj

▸ Lawyers.com. (2012). How, and how much, do lawyers charge?
Retrieved from: http://research.lawyers.com/How-and-How-Much-
Do-Lawyers-Charge.html

▸ Lobb, A. (2005, September). Eating habits – a look at the average
U.S. diet. *The Wall Street Journal Online*. Retrieved from: http://
online.wsj.com/article/SB112671039063140472.html

▸ Luhby, T. (2011). Record number of Americans get government help.
Retrieved from: http://money.cnn.com/2011/04/12/news/economy/
government_safety_net/index.htm

▸ Mackey, J. (2009, August 14). Health care reform – full article.
Retrieved from: http://www2.wholefoodsmarket.com/blogs/
jmackey/2009/08/14/health-care-reform-full-article

▸ Malcom, H. (2012, April 24). Millennials struggle with financial
literacy. *USA Today*. Retrieved from: http://www.usatoday.
com/money/perfi/basics/story/2012-04-23/millenials-financial-
knowledge/54494856/1

▸ Mann, D. (2012). CDC: Americans living longer as death rate
drops. Retrieved from: http://www.medicinenet.com/script/main/art.
asp?articlekey=153546

▸ Marcus, Jon. (2013, February 26) Community college grads out-
earn bachelor's degree holders. CNN Money. Retrieved from: http://
money.cnn.com/2013/02/26/pf/college/community-college-earnings/

▸ Marklein, M. B. (2013). Study: Nearly half are overqualified for their
jobs. *USA Today*. Retrieved from: http://www.usatoday.com/story/
news/nation/2013/01/27/study-nearly-half-are-overqualified-for-
jobs/1868817/

▸ Marquit, M. (2012). Is a graduate degree worth the money?
Retrieved from: http://www.bargaineering.com/articles/graduate-
degree-worth-money.html

▸ Mason, H. (2012). Retrieved from: http://www.youtube.com/watch?v=
EW5IdwltaAc&feature=youtu.be

▸ Mayo Clinic Staff. (2012). Type 2 diabetes. Retrieved from: http://www.mayoclinic.com/health/type-2-diabetes/DS00585

▸ McCloud, L. M. (2006, June 1). Top reasons people divorce: is divorce in the back of your mind as you are saying "i do". Retrieved from: http://voices.yahoo.com/top-reasons-people-divorce-41260.html

▸ McDonald, K. (2001). The cost of a divorce. Retrieved from: http://www.bankrate.com/brm/news/advice/19990903a.asp

▸ McKinsey & Company - McKinsey Center for Government. (2013). Education to employment: Designing a system that works. Retrieved from: http://mckinseyonsociety.com/downloads/reports/Education/Education-to-Employment_FINAL.pdf

▸ Morse, R. and Flanigan, S. (2011, September 12). How *U.S. News* calculates the college rankings. Retrieved from: http://www.usnews.com/education/best-colleges/articles/2011/09/12/how-us-news-calculates-the-college-rankings-2012?page=2

▸ n.a. (2011). 9 alarming U.S. consumer debt statistics. Retrieved from: http://articles.businessinsider.com/2011-05-23/markets/30101275_1_consumer-debt-credit-cards-student-loans

▸ n.a. (2012). Prescription drug deaths. Retrieved from: http://thebalanceyouneed.com/health-wellness/disease-prevention-health-wellness/prescription-drug-deaths

▸ National Consortium on Stigma and Empowerment. (2010). Retrieved from: http://www.stigmaandempowerment.org/

▸ National Institute on Mental Health (2014). The numbers count: Mental disorders in America. Retrieved from: http://www.nimh.nih.gov/health/publications/the-numbers-count-mental-disorders-in-america/index.shtml

▸ NW3C. (2012). National Public Survey on White Collar Crime. Retrieved from: http://www.nw3c.org/research/national_public_survey.cfm

▸ Park, A. (2012). Physicians groups call for fewer tests for patients. Retrieved from: http://healthland.time.com/2012/04/05/physicians-groups-call-for-fewer-tests-for-patients

▸ Parker, K. (2011). College education doesn't prepare for real-life jobs. Retrieved from: http://www.winonadailynews.com/news/opinion/editorial/columnists/article_afa4226c-ef7d-11e0-8c6d-001cc4c03286.html

▸ Petrecca, L. (2010). Toughest test comes after graduation: Getting a job. *USA Today* (June, 21, 2010).

▸ Rampell, C. (2011). Economix: A History of College Grade Inflation. Retrieved from: http://economix.blogs.nytimes.com/2011/07/14/the-history-of-college-grade-inflation/?_php=true&_type=blogs&_r=0

▸ Reynolds, G. H. (2014). Degrees of value: Making college pay off. Retrieved from: http://online.wsj.com/news/articles/SB100014240 52702303870704579298302637802002?mod=WSJ_WSJ_Careers_ CJEducation_2

▸ Rodrik, D. (2013). IMF Survey: Economic Structural Change Vital to Successful Development. Retrieved from: http://www.imf.org/ external/pubs/ft/survey/so/2013/INT062813A.htm

▸ Ronan, G. B. (2005). College freshman face major dilemma. Retrieved from: http://www.msnbc.msn.com/id/10154383/ns/ business-personal_finance/t/college-freshmen-face-major-dilemma

▸ Salary.com. (2012). Search US salaries. Retrieved from: http:// salary.com/category/salary/

▸ Sayers, Mark. (2012). *The Road Trip that Changed the World*. Chicago: Moody Publishers.

▸ Schwartz, L. M. & Woloshin, S. (2012). Endless screenings don't bring everlasting health. [Essay]. *The New York Times*. Retrieved from: http://www.nytimes.com/2012/04/17/health/views/endless-screenings-dont-bring-everlasting-health.html

▸ Seaman, Donna. (2010). Booklist Review of *The Shallows*. Retrieved from: http://www.booklistonline.com/The-Shallows-What-the-Internet-Is-Doing-to-Our-Brains-Nicholas-Carr/pid=4063118

▸ Snyder, M. (2011). 50 things every American should know about the collapse of the economy. Retrieved from: http://www.businessinsider. com/collapse-of-the-economy-2011-5

▸ Sofsian, D. (2007). Obesity statistics. Retrieved from: http:// ezinearticles.com/?Obesity-Statistics&id=405478

▸ Student Debt and the Class of 2012. (2014). Project on Student Debt. Retrieved from: http://projectonstudentdebt.org/ files/pub/ classof2012.pdf

▸ The Chronicle of Higher Education. (2012). Business leaders say they're underwhelmed by the college graduates they hire. Retrieved from: http://chronicle.com/blogs/ticker/business-leaders-say-theyreunderwhelmed-by-college-graduates-seeking-jobs/39997

▸ The Institute for Social Health Innovation Policy. (2010). Social health index. Retrieved from: http://iisp.vassar.edu/ish.html

▸ Top 10 College Majors (2014). Retrieved from: http://www.princetonreview.com/college/top-ten-majors.aspx

▸ Turkle, S. (2012, May 28). We expect more from technology and less from each other. Retrieved from http://www.cnn.com/2012/05/27/opinion/turkle-ted-technology/

▸ U.S. national debt clock. (2014, March). Retrieved from: http://www.usdebtclock.org

▸ UNC Charlotte and University City. (2009). Employers desire soft skills from college graduates. Retrieved from: http://uncc49er.com/518/employers-desire-soft-skills-from-college-graduates

▸ Graves, J. (2014). The best jobs of 2014. Retrieved from: http://money.usnews.com/money/careers/ articles/2014/01/23/the-best-jobs-of-2014

▸ Vedder, R. (2012, January). Beware: alternative certification is coming. Retrieved from: http://chronicle.com/blogs/innovations/beware-alternative-certification-is-coming/31369

▸ Wadsworth, G. H. (2011). Sky rocketing college costs. Retrieved from: http://inflationdata.com/inflation/inflation_articles/Education_Inflation.asp

▸ Watson, B. (2011). Graduating from college? Hope you learned how to tend bar. Retrieved from: http://www.dailyfinance.com/2011/11/29/graduating-from-college-hope-you-learned-how-to-tend-bar

▸ Watson, B. (2012). Student loan, meet Social Security. Retrieved from: http://www.dailyfinance.com/2012/05/01/student-loans-meet-social-security-seniors-stuck-school-debt

▸ White, M.C. (2013). The real reason new college grads can't get hired. Retrieved from: http://business.time.com/2013/11/10/the-real-reason-new-college-grads-cant-get-hired/#ixzz2wLB83qT8

▸ Will, G. (2009, January 11). Litigious society lacks common sense. Retrieved from: http://www2.ljworld.com/news/2009/jan/11/litigious-society-lacks-common-sense/

▸ Woolsey, B., & Gerson, E. S. (2009). The history of credit cards. Retrieved from: http://www.creditcards.com/credit-card-news/credit-cards-history-1264.php

▸ Yen, H. (2012, April 23). Weak labor market even weaker for college grads. *The Dallas Morning News*, 5A.

▸ Yerak, B. (2012, April 22). College paybacks, ad infinitum. *The Dallas Morning News*, 23A.

The Mobile App

✦ Free to download

✦ Free video lectures

✦ Full subscriber access

Search for: Acceleron Learning

Developed by Subsplash